Echoes in Ferryland

Potomac River

Westmoreland County

Richmond County

Northumberland County

Lancaster County

Rappahannock River

Chesapeake Bay

N

The Northern Neck of Virginia

ISBN: 978-0-9838264-2-2
Library of Congress Control Number: 2011939597

Printed in the United States

Belle Isle Books
belleislebooks.com

Echoes in Ferryland

A Remembrance of Virginia's Northern Neck

by

Nancy Hubbard Clark

Belle Isle Books

To the memory of my dear husband, Irwin, who traded life in his native North Carolina for my Northern Neck of Virginia.

And to our children, Charles, Mark, and Cameron, so they may know the people and places of their Virginia heritage and because they listened patiently as I rattled on and on with my stories.

To our grandchildren who, hopefully, may someday enjoy hearing how life was lived in my time on this "Neck" of land.

Finally, to the memory of my parents, who lovingly provided me with a rich and happy childhood; and to all of the dear folks who surrounded me with small yet wondrous experiences.

Contents

Acknowledgments

My heartfelt gratitude goes to Sylvia Kilduff Ball for reading my first draft and for her support, advice, and encouragement. She has been my mentor throughout the project, giving me the courage and impetus for publishing these sketches. My first intent was only to make a recording for my children.

I am indebted to Jeanne Rose, who could read my longhand and type all of it for me, patiently and expertly throughout my many changes and additions, and for making the process such a pleasure for me.

For his knowledge and expertise, I am eternally grateful to John C. Wilson for proofreading. My thanks to him also for his permission to copy a few photos from his book, *Virginia's Northern Neck, a pictorial history*.

My gratitude also goes to Lee Rice, Ed Layman and Marty Taylor, who offered some tips on publishing.

For other valuable contributions I owe thanks to Lorena Dobyns Conner, Margaret Ransone, Eleanor Hayden, and my cousin Meredith McKenney for their memory that the hotel in Lancaster was operated only by the Beane family; and also to my cousin Bob Lee Covington and his wife, Gene, for relating his mother's amusing hotel story to me.

To cousin Janet Beane Davenport, who supplied "Hob" Davenport's full name as well as information concerning Uncle Archie's second tomato factory.

To Rosemary Tomlin for giving me the last name of "Aunt Janie" Kenner.

To Bernice Culver Shelly for providing information about the early days of White Stone Beach and its sliding board "secret."

To Augusta Eubank Sellew for contributing the information on my dad's Kilmarnock Town Council service and the use of some photos at the Kilmarnock Museum.

To Virginia and Bob Fleet, who supplied the name of Winnie Abbott, the popular fishing party captain of my memory.

To Bud (I. M.) Bussells for providing his family's World War II military service information.

To Bertram Chase for his naval service information.

To Helen Layman Quillan for helping to fill in some of the tricentennial story.

To Denise Hughes Elias for the photo of Jackie Hughes.

To Rhea Frances Talley for the treasured street photo of Jeanne Blake and me.

To Betty Jo Venable Covington for White Stone Beach photos.

To cousin Ann C. Green Carver for contributing the lost ballet picture of me, found in her mother's (my Aunt Lucy's) memorabilia.

To *The Rappahannock Record* for use of the photo of the *Miss Virginia* ferryboat taken by William Haislip.

Credit also goes to the booklet *The Way We Came Together; Lancaster County During World War II*, by Cathy Curry, published by the Mary Ball Washington Museum and Library for information concerning the plane spotter paraphernalia and the British sailors training on the river here.

The souvenir program of the Lancaster County Tricentennial was my source for some of the information concerning that event.

Introduction

As a native of the lower Northern Neck of Virginia—a "born here"—I've also spent most of my life living on this peninsula where my roots run deep in the land between the two rivers that flow into the Chesapeake Bay.

Now in my later years I'm prompted to record some of my experiences that were shaped by life as we knew it in the time between the coming of the two bridges at each end of the "Neck." The advent of these structures marked vast changes in lifestyle throughout the area.

I'm sure that the activities of my childhood and young adult life may seem amusing or boring in relation to more modern or wider experiences. Yet, I do feel that my story may provoke a certain kind of yen for this simpler way of life and the unabashed naïvete that came with it. All of these memories are true to the pictures etched in my mind—with no embellishments or alterations to distort their authenticity. I have not attempted to create a fine literary composition. This is merely a set of recollections transcribed straight from my heart.

I

God's Country

The Northern Neck of Virginia is a peninsula that has been a virtual island unto itself since its settlement in the seventeenth century. With its great beauty guarded by its natural situation, the "Neck" juts out from the mainland—cut off by water on three sides: the Rappahannock River, the Potomac River, and Chesapeake Bay at its tip. Owing to this, no major battles were fought in the area. The people here remained in relative isolation—most of them choosing not to leave their tranquil paradise.

The passage of time, the Civil War, and the Great Depression caused a lengthy period when wealth was a condition known to very few, though natives were rich in pride and spirit. They were wise to seek education and ways to take advantage of the opportunities that this unique peninsula offered. Their discoveries of ways to use the land and water provided a good life—apart from the sophistication of an outside world. The "sweet-life" was enjoyed in modest ways, with its limitations dictated by the circumstances of each point in time. They loved the place and didn't want to leave. They called their paradise "God's Country." The soul of the true native "Northern Necker" has always been imbued with a gentle spirit of warmth, honesty, hospitality, and concern for others.

In the early nineteen fifties, when the Honorable Blake T. Newton of Westmoreland County delivered an address to crown a Holly Ball queen, he remarked that "natives who leave the Northern Neck are always angling to find a way to return to 'God's Country'."

II

Labor Day Child

In 1927 the Downing Bridge opened at Tappahannock in Essex County, crossing the Rappahannock River to the shores of the Northern Neck on the Warsaw side. This marked the arrival of the first easy gateway to the peninsula.

My parents married in 1928 and the Great Depression began in 1929, just before I was born.

In the twenties my dad had been a student at the College of William and Mary. Mother had first been a student at Blackstone College for Girls—until it burned—and later at Fredericksburg State Normal School (now the University of Mary Washington). She was a hometown girl and after their marriage refused the idea of a move to Norfolk where my dad thought of going for employment. Therefore, in 1928 he bravely set out in Lancaster County to establish himself in the insurance business. His daily travels took him up and down the length of the Northern Neck, where he worked to cultivate clientele for his fledgling business. This was just about the time when the Great Depression began, which affected the economic condition of the entire nation. He worked hard all through those tough years and managed to become successful. He named the business Hubbard Insurance Agency, Inc.

I arrived on the scene on Labor Day weekend in 1930. My birth was to be quite enough for the young couple, who were suddenly launched into Depression Era parenthood. I became their only child.

Dr. B. H. B. Hubbard—my grandfather's cousin—delivered me at home on Irvington Road in Kilmarnock. It must have been quite an eventful day because my parents never thought to give me a middle name. All of my life this has been a source of much regret for me. There were many nice family names on the "tree", but they gave me only one name. Mother always said that I was a "ten month baby." Evidently it had been a long hot summer for her and my birth a rather traumatic delivery, although I never heard it discussed. I only remember her talking about Mrs. Dix, the nurse who continued to stay at our home for quite a long while following my birth.

Whenever I expressed my wish for a middle name Mother said, "Girls drop their middle names when they marry." I was glad that she had so much confidence in my future. I guess it was part of the reasoning on that eventful day, but nonetheless, I was disappointed in the short little name that they had given to me. I felt shortchanged. Many times in my childhood I added a middle one when I put my name in the books I owned. I often signed my name as "Nancy Rebekah Hubbard" or "Nancy Carter Hubbard." After all, I thought, it was only natural that I should be like all of my friends whose names sounded so pretty.

III

Roots 'n' All

Mother

My mother's name was Rebekah Stakes Beane. She was the youngest child of her father's second family of seven children by my grandmother. Aunt Celeste and Mother always laughed that "Rebekah was named for Papa's first wife because he had run out of names by the time she was born." He had four children by his first wife.

Grandpapa's name was William George Beane. He had been known respectfully as "Mr. W. G. Beane," for he was well thought of in the community. At the end of the Civil War he served as a young Confederate soldier and, luckily, was never wounded.

Upon returning after the war he became engaged in farming and the lumber business, acquiring large tracts of timberland in Northumberland County and the upper reaches of Lancaster County. He also became owner and operator of the hotel in the village of Lancaster, where court days made the hotel a bustling establishment. He was a member of the County Board of Supervisors and was the pillar of nearby Edgely Methodist-Episcopal Church. Grandpapa was a staunch Methodist and played a leading role in the operation of the Methodists' Marvin Grove Church Camp that convened each August in the Heathsville area.

My mother and her sisters loved to talk about those times at "Marvin Grove Camp meeting." Their family "tent" was one of nearly a hundred small frame houses that were set around the central open-air tabernacle where evening religious services were held. They talked of promenading around the grounds, of eating ice cream, of meeting friends, and of the planning they did each year for taking new clothes to "camp meeting." Marvin Grove was one of three church camps in the lower Northern Neck and was attended by three or four thousand people during its

4

August session. The camp burned in 1930. The others were Wharton Grove (Baptist) at Weems and Kirkland Grove (Baptist), also near Heathsville.

Edgely Church's small congregation died out soon after Grandpapa's death in 1922 and the church closed its doors forever. The frame building was still standing, empty, in the 1940s when Mother and her sister, Celeste, made trips there to tend the family burial plot. My cousin, Gerry Cooper, and I went with our mothers on these trips. We even played "church" inside of the old empty building while our mothers worked outside. We found

Mother with her sisters and friends at the Beane family cottage at Marvin Grove Camp, 1919.

some old hymn books scattered askew on the floor of the barren sanctuary and used them to conduct our "service." Many years later the church was razed. Today the churchyard remains vacant except for the graveyard, which, shamefully, is now a forgotten and neglected site.

One of Grandpapa's children—by his first wife—was his daughter, Allie, who married Mr. James W. G. Stephens of Wicomico Church, Virginia. Their son, Ennolls Albert Stephens, later known as "Big Steve," built The Tides Inn at Irvington in 1947. The Inn attracted many outsiders to the Northern Neck and was the impetus for expanded development here in the Neck following World War II. It is interesting to note that Big Steve's grandfather Beane (also my grandfather) had also owned a hotel, though far removed in time, style, size, and purpose—the old hotel at Lancaster C. H.

Grandpapa's second wife was my grandmother, Mary Annie Robertson, known as "Annie." I called her "Mee-Ma." Her family had come from the Eastern Shore of Maryland. Her sister, Ella, who lived in Baltimore, was an artist as well as a hat designer for Hothschild-Kohn department store in Baltimore. There were oil paintings in the family done by Aunt

Ella, as well as a wax water lily sculpture, under a glass dome, which was a popular Victorian craft art. I remember it well— and also an old Beaver hat that she had sent to my mother. I wore the hat when I played "long dresses." She must have been an interesting lady. Aunt Ella came to visit occasionally, but I was too young to remember her.

Mother's siblings were Archie, Harry, Ruth, Marie, Olivia, and Celeste.

Archie (Archibald Robertson B.) who, following his college years at Randolph Macon College in Ashland, Va., served in the Army during

Mee-Ma," my grandmother Beane.

World War I. After the war he came home and became engaged in farming and forestry, as his papa had done, and also operated two tomato canneries. He served as county treasurer for many years.

Harry (Harry Clay B.) owned the Chrysler/Plymouth dealership, known as "Standard Motors," in Kilmarnock. He married Margaret Wheary of Petersburg, Virginia, who came to the county in the forties to teach high school.

Ruth married Virgil McKenney and, as a widow, operated the hotel in Lancaster for many years following Papa's death. She attended Chesapeake Academy.

Marie and Olivia also attended the first Chesapeake Academy in Irvington and married brothers from Northumberland County. Marie married Roland E. Covington and Olivia married R. Lee Covington.

Celeste taught school for many years after attending Fredericksburg State Normal School. She was always a strong advocate of education. Unfortunately, her young husband, Lynn E. Cooper, died suddenly on Christmas day in 1945.

The Village

Mother's home was in Lancaster Court House—the county seat—where I spent many happy times visiting the family. Grandpapa moved his large family there from the farm that had been located about ten miles from Lancaster in order to be close to the school, which was just outside of the village. He bought the house in the village that had once been the Methodist parsonage—probably because of his strong affiliation with Edgely Methodist Church. The communion silver that he had provided for the church later came back into the family after Edgely Church closed. Many years afterward I inherited the set from my mother and gave it to the Mary Ball Washington Museum in Lancaster. It was a typical Victorian set of quadruple plate silver, consisting of four pieces: a tall urn (ewer); a pair of chalices (goblets on stem); and a small round tray (the paten).

My early memories of the sweet, quiet courthouse village are mostly of its people, the special old buildings, and the large old sycamore trees.

In the summertime those trees shaded its only street, the main highway that ran straight through the heart of the village. In autumn they created a scene of large ugly brown leaves swirling and blowing everywhere. As the pesky leaves began to overtake front yards and the sidewalk along the street, the villagers raked them into regularly spaced piles beside the edge of the road and burned them. Riding through the hamlet at that time of the year was like traveling through a colossal smokescreen.

In the thirties and forties traffic was almost nonexistent on the highway. Whenever we sat on the front porch at

Edgely Church communion set.

the Beane home we could count as few as a dozen cars passing by in a single afternoon.

The old brick jail was painted white and sat across the road from the courthouse. In the thirties it still housed a few inmates who could be heard giving an occasional yell or two from windows of the ground floor cells where they were being held. This was a spooky curiosity to us children and we were afraid to go anywhere near the jail. We cautiously investigated though, daring to sneak across the field—keeping a safe distance from the jail. We always scurried away in excitement whenever we heard one of the prisoners yell, but soon repeated the sneaking, over and over, like a relay

The Lancaster Jail at Lancaster Courthouse, 1930s. *Photo courtesy of the Library of Virginia.*

game. This was high drama entertainment for us on a quiet summer day.

On one side of the courthouse front yard—the side closest to the old post office and a tall sycamore tree—the remnants of the platform base of the ancient colonial stocks were still in place. About the time of the remodeling of the courthouse in 1939 Gerry and I once "made believe" we were prisoners and played on it because the grown-ups had told me stories of how the stocks were used. The idea immediately sounded exciting so

I proceeded, with great relish, to enlist my little cousin for the enactment of our version of the penalty scene. We were very young—probably nine- and four-year olds—but I do remember playing "prisoner" on the base of the platform of the old stocks.

My grandmother, Annie Beane, operated the hotel after Grandpapa's death in 1922 and then her daughter, Ruth B. McKenney (my aunt), operated the Hotel from 1926 until 1938. At that time Mr. Jim Giese had a small store at one end of the hotel building. It was never a part of the hotel operation. Giese's store was next to the small frame post office—now known as the Blakemore building—at the edge of the courthouse yard. When my family operated the old hotel it had a large dining room at the rear of the structure with the kitchen located behind it. My cousin, Meredith McKenney, lived at the hotel in the years when his mother, Ruth, was operating it. He remembered that the original kitchen had been in the yard, behind and away from the building. It was finally brought up and attached to the hotel at the rear of the dining room. I vividly remember stepping down from the front hall into the dining room that was filled with tables. This was sometime before the large rear section of the building

The hotel at Lancaster as it appeared in the 1930s. Drawn by the author.

was removed in the early 1940s. The hotel closed and ceased operation after Ruth McKenney sold the building in 1938 to James Cornwell. Mr. Giese's sister, from Baltimore, soon bought the building from Mr. Cornwell and it then became the Giese home. Mr. Giese continued to run his store, offering snack bar items, soft drinks, and emergency supplies, as well as selling gas from the tank located in front of his store.

One family hotel story that my mother's sister, Olivia, told many times was about meeting her future husband at the hotel. Olivia's story was of playing the piano there and singing—with her sister, Maryee—that then-popular old song, "There's a long, long trail awinding—into the land of my dreams —." Then, on a chance visit to the village, Lee Covington and his brother decided to stop in at the hotel. When they came through the front door, Lee joined in the singing (he had a nice tenor voice). Olivia and Lee had never met, but Olivia always said that she knew she would marry him from the moment of that first musical encounter! Her children were always amused by her romantic reverie, which she repeatedly told to them. When she married Lee Covington in 1915 their wedding was held at White Marsh Methodist Church, a lovely old county landmark that stands idle today (in 2009) with no congregation. It sits by the side of Route 3 between Lancaster and Kilmarnock, at the former location of Brookvale post office.

The Confederate monument, encircled by its iron fence, is still located in a prominent central spot in the village. It stands beside the highway and is close to the old clerk's office. Grandpapa's name is on it, along with several of my other relatives. Both my mother and Aunt Celeste were members of the U. D. C. (United Daughters of the Confederacy), which was a very active organization here in the 1930s.

Mrs. Gresham's house stood just behind the monument, with its front screened porch facing the monument and the street. Elizabeth and Louis Hammock lived there with her mother. Elizabeth was a lovely soft-spoken lady, always perfectly groomed, stylishly dressed, and a person of notable gracious manners. Her husband, Louis—ever the proper gentleman—operated his tomato cannery "up the country." Elizabeth was a distant relative of mine, on my father's side of the family. She served as mistress of ceremonies for my wedding in 1955. I was especially fond of her.

Mrs. Carney's house stood next to Trinity Episcopal Church. Mrs. Carney was the former Mary Gresham. She'd been described as "Lily of the Forest" in the orator's coronation address when she was crowned Holly Ball Queen in 1900, for she was a beautiful and charming lady. Perhaps the "forest" referred to the large number of sycamore trees that grew in the area at the time, or perhaps it was because the village was not near the river. The "forest" term is debatable.

Mrs. Carney's home, with its upper and lower porches extending across the full length of the front of the house, was aligned so that one end of the house was parallel to the street and the front of the house faced the Confederate monument. The house had formerly served as the rectory for

Christ Church Parish. Trinity Church in Lancaster Court House is midway between St. Mary's White Chapel and Grace Church. The three churches then made up Christ Church Parish. When Trinity was built in 1884 it was erected facing the street, which made one of its sides oriented to the rear of the rectory. Some years after Mrs. Carney's death the house was abandoned and was finally razed following years of decline. Today (in 2009) the church parking lot occupies the space where the large old house once stood.

My aunt, Celeste, my uncle, Archie, and Archie's family all became members of Trinity Church. Trinity was where I attended a wedding for the first time in my life. My dad's cousin, Olivia Ball Carter, was married there to John Harrison and it became a memorable event for me. I was about five or six years old and remember eagerly watching for the bride and her attendants to enter through the doorway and file down the aisle going past the pew where I sat with my parents. I was thrilled at this part of the wedding, but was shocked into fright later at the reception. There were candles burning on the table where the bride and groom cut the wedding cake at her home. Suddenly, as Olivia Ball turned, candle flames nearly caught the tulle of her wedding veil. There was a flurry of excitement and people moved about quickly in the room. The greatest of disasters was narrowly avoided, but my fright over the incident never faded and I've always been intimidated by the use of candles.

The Davenport family home is located across the street from Trinity Church. In the early forties a handsome black iron fence still surrounded the yard of the home. "Hob" Davenport (John Hobson D.) had operated a large general store in the space between the hotel and the old tavern. His daughter-in-law, Irene Davenport (Mrs. J. Gilliam D.), continued living in the home for many years after her husband's death, rearing her sons, Jack and Jimmy, there. When her sons were serving in the Army during World War II, she joined the Women's Army Corps (W. A. C.) to do her part for the "war effort" as well. She was a very noble and strong person. After the war she returned to the home to live out her long and inspiring life of good nature and fortitude.

Up the street, near the old jail, was where "Treenie" (Katherine) Pierce lived during World War II—and afterward until her death. Her first husband, "Chit" (Chichester) Pierce, had gone to war and was killed at the

Battle of the Bulge, leaving Treenie with their very young son. She was an outstanding character of towering strength with a sparkling and subtle sense of humor that made her widely popular. She and Irene Davenport became sworn friends. When Irene was housebound in her later years, Treenie walked down the street to Irene's each morning at eleven o'clock to play a game of "Spite and Malice." It was their special card game of "fun for two" and was a morning ritual that was well known to everyone in the village.

My aunt, Celeste, and Irene were also great friends. The village was more like one big family than just a place with townspeople. Another of Treenie's close friends was Lorena Dobyns Conner. The Dobyns family operated a cannery in the Monaskon area. Lorena was the county commissioner of the revenue for many years and was like a member of the village "gentry." She took many trips with Treenie in later life. Several years after the end of the war, Treenie married "Ran" (W. Ransdell Chilton) and they were happily married for many years. Then, as a widow once more, Treenie became the founder of the Mary Ball Washington Museum and Library in the village. She was public-spirited and very interested in preserving the history of Lancaster County. Mary Ball was born in upper Lancaster County and, after her marriage to Augustine Washington, became the mother of George, our nation's first president. The museum was named in her honor.

Dr. Oldham's home was the small ancient white cottage, with a cedar-thatched roof, next to the Beane home, on the side of the street directly opposite the Confederate Monument. His tiny white office building was on the other side of his home, toward the tavern. He used this office for night hours in the village.

Dr. Oldham had an old shaggy brown and black dog named "Chocolate," his faithful companion. Chocolate was always at his side, and they were a widely recognized pair throughout the entire county. He also had a young driver for his small Ford car. This fellow, "Merry" Jones, was a handsome, light-complected, very mannerly black man who drove Dr. Oldham and Chocolate on housecalls or wherever the doctor went. After all, the good doctor would not be the safest driver to meet on the highway. It seemed that he was known to enjoy a toddy or two on occasion.

Apparently Dr. Oldham cared little for grooming or style. He never appeared dressed in anything other than his tired, brown, pinstriped baggy suit and a floppy, well-worn, dark felt hat. The short little gentleman, of slight build, had a kind face with a wrinkled complexion and discerning blue eyes. He spoke in a low and gravelly voice when he came to our house to dispense the annual "spring-cleaning" pills to children such as me. These little brown pills never failed to "do the job" and were supposed to ensure good health for the entire coming year.

His main office was a gray frame building on Waverly Avenue in Kilmarnock. There his many cats dominated the scene, roaming throughout the office and onto the examining table until shooed off by one wide sweep of his arm. Nevertheless, Dr. Oldham was a well-loved and very respected gentleman who was known to everyone as a very smart man.

His wife, "Miss Sadie," was the daughter of Reverend Combs of Trinity Church. Their niece, "Toodles," lived with them. Toodles was a high-spirited and jolly girl who was often seen driving gaily through the village in the family car wearing a hat set at a rakish angle on her head. She was a good bit older than I, but somehow Toodles made a lasting impression on my young mind. Her nickname was probably a part of the reason why I remember her so well.

There was a back lot behind the Oldham home where a small chicken house stood. Sometimes, from my Aunt Celeste's house that was next door to the Oldhams', we could hear a great burst of commotion erupting in the back lot. This was when one of the hens was flapping its wings and squawking violently in a hopeless attempt to avoid the blows of a falling ax. The first stage of preparations had begun for the hen to become the featured course on the Oldhams' dinner menu that night. The flurry of activity always came and went in short, pulsating spurts until silence suddenly fell and announced the end of the agonizing torture.

Lila and Oscar Chilton lived up the street in the house with brown shingle siding that had been a tavern in "olden times." Their tavern/home stood across the road from the colonial brick clerk's office, which had been built in 1797. Oscar was the county clerk; Lila was a daughter of Dr. Combs, the much-revered rector of Trinity Church and Christchurch Parish. Lila was always seen wearing a scarf wrapped tightly around her head, tied in headband fashion. A monocle dangled around her neck. She had a rather feisty disposition and certain definite opinions, which she often freely expressed, at times using a very colorful vocabulary. The villagers all seemed to understand Lila's nature. It was said that she enjoyed an afternoon "nip" on a regular basis after spending most of her day reading books. I was afraid of their bulldog that barked furiously whenever we walked past the house and was glad that they kept that scary dog on the porch.

The Cornwell family lived in the old frame house near the clerk's office. It's now the Mary Ball Washington Museum and Library. Jimmy Cornwell operated his general store and sold gas at the frame building next to his home. The Lancaster County Women's Club now occupies that building. Cornwell's store was the central grocery market between Kilmarnock and the upper part of the county in the 1930s and 40s. It had succeeded Davenport's Store of earlier days. Whenever I visited and spent time in Lancaster with Aunt Celeste, I often played doll babies and "paper dolls" with Jane, his daughter, who was near my age. We always had great fun together. Sometimes we cut our paper dolls from a Sears Roebuck catalog. Jane was always my partner in the jail sneaking expeditions.

There was another person in Lancaster who always fascinated me. She was my uncle Archie's wife, Berta Mae. She was from Roanoke, Virginia. He had met her when he was serving in the Army during World War I. Her family, the Moomaws, was a well-known family of that area who were quite the antique connoisseurs. Berta Mae, usually called "Mae," had an attic that she had filled to capacity with antiques. One time I saw her attic and remember the excitement that overtook me when I saw all of those "old timey" things. It was like a step back into another age for a little girl such as I. Naturally, she had furnished their home with nice antique furniture. I especially liked their grandfather clock.

Mae was an extremely thrifty person who loved antique bargain hunting, but she refused to spend money on clothes. Her penny pinching, in that respect, was a source of amazement to my mother and Aunt Celeste. They knew that their brother could well afford for her to buy more clothes. But dressing was not her prime interest. She cared more about buying antiques and seemed to know exactly where the best "find" could be located. She, indeed, was a very savvy antique collector. I'm sure that her warm and genial nature was advantageous to her whenever she made desirable antique discoveries.

Spending a few days in Lancaster with Aunt Celeste also meant that she would be sure that Gerry and I paid a visit to the Bookmobile when it made its periodic stop in the village. She let us help her select books, which she read to us either at bedtime or as we sat on the front porch in the afternoon.

I remember the day when Gerry and I sneaked into Uncle Archie's garage that was next door to Aunt Celeste's (the Beane home) and where Grandpapa's old Model T Ford car was stored. We were amazed when we looked inside and saw the bright blue velvet interior of that funny automobile. So we promptly climbed up onto the running board and got inside to make believe we were driving. Now we could take a trip far out into the great wide world. I allowed Gerry to sit behind the wheel and do the driving. It was a grandiose gesture of kindness and generosity on my part—owing to the seniority in age that I had over my little cousin. After all, I was five years older.

Often on Sunday nights Mother, Daddy, and I had supper with Aunt Celeste's family. The baked capon chicken dinners were usually followed by her delicious lemon meringue pie—my favorite dessert. On these nights Gerry and I played board games with the family. The games were usually Chinese checkers, Parcheesi, or Monopoly.

In the early thirties our family celebrated the Fourth of July in the village by having a picnic and then a fireworks display when darkness came. The fireworks were the kind that were hand-held and were shot into the air by some brave adult male member of the family. Gerry and I could hardly wait for nightfall because it was always an exciting time for us. We loved being allowed to hold and twirl the sparklers. As part of the Fourth celebration during World War II, he and I dressed up patriotically as a soldier and a nurse to have our picture taken. Another time during the forties, the entire family celebrated the Fourth at Westmoreland State Park. It was a full day outing of picnic, swimming, and fireworks. Fried chicken and potato salad were on the picnic menu, of course, along with chocolate cake and watermelon.

During the early 1940s Jimmy Davenport was attending Christchurch School, near Urbanna in Middlesex County. On one of his visits home he brought a record, which we played on the hand-cranked Victrola at Aunt Celeste's house. The tune was "String of Pearls." It was the first time that I had ever heard the Glenn Miller band and right away I loved it. I was about twelve years old and secretly began to eye Jimmy with an early crush developing. He was seventeen.

A trip outside of the village—to Uncle Archie's tomato cannery—opened up a whole different view of village life. The factory was situated just outside of Lancaster, down the hill from the courthouse and around the big curve.

Inside, the cannery was a scene of loud machine noises and frantic activity with heavy clouds of steam filling the air under the roof of the open-sided building. It looked to me like the tomatoes were being boiled in huge vats of water. Then quickly they were put into large metal bowls sitting on long tables in front of black women who stood working at the tables. They deftly peeled the scalded tomatoes and filled cans that rolled along in front of them on tracks propelled by rotating belts. Then the cans were delivered on these tracks to a station where the lids were finally popped in place by a lid-capping machine. Though sweating and working in the ferocious heat of this environment, many of the women sang Gospel songs. At the time when I witnessed this noisy, steamy scene I was about ten or eleven years old. It was a view of activity that was unforgettable and made a lasting impression on my young mind.

Tomato canneries were fairly numerous throughout the Neck in the 1940s. It was a productive industry for the area. Uncle Archie's brand label was "Mantua." That name came from the Mantua voting district in Lancaster County at the time. His other cannery was located on the old road to Lively (Route 201), in the building that is now occupied (2009) by the United Parcel Service.

Daddy

My dad's name was Charles Walton Hubbard, Jr. He was known all of his life as "Charlie," but I called him "Daddy Charlie" when I was very young. He called me "my pal" at first and later, "Pig" or "Sugar Pig," which was his term of endearment for me—with none of the modern connotation of ugliness attached to it. After all, I was "Daddy's little girl."

My dad insisted that I learn certain things. Among them was his requirement that I be a good sport.

On my twelfth birthday I was apparently a poor sport and very saucy when I was playing a game of croquet in the yard at Waterview Farm with all of the family, which included my aunt and uncle. Daddy decided that I needed correcting for my ugliness, so he reached for a twig from the big maple tree to show his disapproval of my behavior. That was the greatest surprise of my young life. He had never switched me for ANYTHING before that day, and it was the only time that it ever happened. In my youth that method of discipline was commonly used to teach children the proper respect for their elders and this was how my dad chose to make the point on that day.

The lesson he gave me in honesty and apologies came one day on the street in Kilmarnock when I was returning from high school. My friend, Jeanne Blake, and I had thought that we were pretty cute by putting salt in the sugar bowls on the tables in Dr. Layman's People's Drugstore. I inadvertently revealed our prank at home. A few days later, when I encountered Daddy conversing on the street with Dr. Layman, my dad called me aside to remind me that I "had something to apologize to Dr. Layman for"—and my knees buckled as I managed to say, "I'm sorry we put salt in the sugar, Dr. Layman."

My dad was like all Virginians who taught their offspring to meet people with a firm handshake and to look them straight in the eye when introduced. This was another must for me to learn.

Daddy's father was C. W. Hubbard, Sr., known as Walton Hubbard, but to the family he was always "Father." Father Hubbard's ancestors had settled on Dymer Creek, a tributary of Fleet's Bay, near the Chesapeake in lower Lancaster County. They settled there around 1770 and called their farm "Apple Grove." The frame house still stands, though barely recognizable today due to a series of tragic renovations done by successive new owners since the 1940s. Father's mother was from the Bartley James family, who settled at Waterview Farm on nearby Antipoison Creek around 1780. Father inherited Waterview from the James side of his family and that is where my dad was born. Father and my grandmother, "Nanee," as she was always known to me, went to live at Waterview after their marriage.

"Nanee," my grandmother Hubbard, as a bride in 1902.

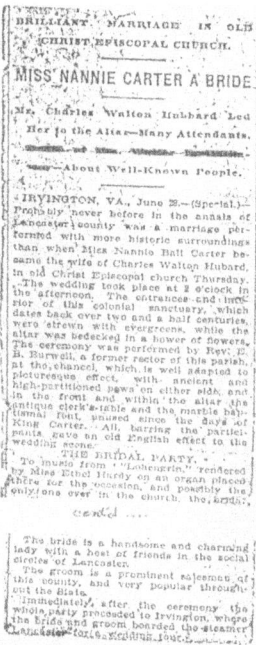

Wedding account in *The Virginia Citizen,* an Irvington, Virginia newspaper.

Nanee's name was Ann Ball Carter, known as "Nannie Carter." They were married in 1902 at Lancaster County's Christ Church, built in 1735, and their marriage was described as an important occasion in this area for the time. It was the first wedding to be held in the old church since the newly formed congregation of the Protestant Episcopal Church had begun to hold occasional services there. The church had suffered a long period of abandonment as a result of the disestablishment of the Anglican Church in the Colonies following the Revolution. In glowing news accounts of their marriage by the *Virginia Citizen*, an Irvington newspaper, and also by a Richmond newspaper, it was reported that an organ had been brought into the church for the first time to provide the wedding music. The news articles also noted that the couple had departed for a "wedding tour" aboard the steamboat *Lancaster*.

Nanee was a descendant of the church's builder, Robert "King" Carter. Her parents were Lucy Olivia Ball and Charles Landon Carter, whose Carters were from the Ball's Neck area of Northumberland County. Her relationship to the Robert Carter family was through the Ball connection to that family, but is much too tedious and unnecessary to explain here. Suffice it to say that early families of the Northern Neck, as well as other Virginia families, married into families close

Nannie and Walton's wedding tour steamer, *Lancaster. Photo courtesy of the Steamboat Era Museum.*

Bewdley, the ancestral Ball family home. *Photo courtesy of Mary Ball Washington Museum and Library, Inc.*

enough to call nearly everyone "cousin."

After the early deaths of both of her parents, Nanee went to live at Greenvale Farm in upper Lancaster County with her aunt Cornelia ("Corie") Carter, who had married Mr. John Robert Chilton. Nanee's Ball family ancestors had lived at Bewdley on Deep Creek, off of the Rappahannock, which was also the home of Mary Ball Washington's relatives. The Balls married into the family of their cousins, the Lees of Ditchley, near Kilmarnock in Northumberland County. Great grandmother, Lucy Olivia Ball, lived at Ditchley with her family. She and great grandfather were married there and later were also buried there. After their marriage they had gone to live at Long Branch, which was the name of their home that was located on a long finger of Indian Creek. Nanee was born there.

Long Branch was located on part of the Clifton land, close to Kilmarnock. Clifton had been inherited by Robert Wormely Carter from his father, Landon Carter, of Sabine Hall in Richmond County. My great grandmother's name, Lucy O. Ball, is shown on an old plat of that land and is evidently the reason why she and her husband settled there. The original part of the Long Branch house is no longer recognizable. The edifice sits back from the road, now Route #608.

When I was a little girl I loved for Nanee to tell me the story that her "Antie" (Corie Carter Chilton) had told her about the Yankees coming to Greenvale and pillaging for grain and farm animals. There were no Civil War battles fought in the area, but Yankees were, indeed, pillaging homes along the river, and Greenvale had been the site of one of these raids. There had been a Yankee encampment in the vicinity of Greenvale and that place eventually became known as "Yankee Point."

A rather amazing discovery about my family connections came to me in the 1980s when my dad's sister, Lucy, came here for her annual summer visit from her home in Natchez, Mississippi. She told me that when she and Daddy were quite young, Antie had come to live at Waterview Farm with Nanee's family following Mr. Chilton's death. Although the Chiltons had no children themselves, they provided a small school at Greenvale where a few families sent their children. My understanding is that this was a fairly common practice since there were no public schools at the time. The Stephens boys—my grandpapa Beane's grandchildren, by the daughter of his first wife—had spent a lot of time as youngsters at Greenvale with Antie and Mr. Chilton. For that reason the young Stephens boys later came to visit Antie at Waterview when she was living there. This odd connecting link between both sides of my family, although not a blood connection, shows how close families of the Neck were sometimes intertwined in various ways.

Nanee had attended the Brockenbrough family's school at their home, Belleville, in Warsaw. That school was known as Brockenbrough Institute and Nanee's older sister, Lucy, taught there. Later Nanee taught school at the small grade school in Kilmarnock. There is a picture at the Kilmarnock Museum of that little one-room school with the schoolchildren and its two teachers: Miss Leolyn Bonner and Miss Nannie Carter (Nanee).

My grandfather attended William and Mary College in the years around 1892 and then became a salesman for a Baltimore pharmaceutical firm. He spent long days and nights away from the Northern Neck, usually on the Middle Peninsula. It must have been difficult traveling with horse and buggy via steamboat and later by ferries to cross the rivers in those early days. Steamer travel ended in 1933 when steamboat wharves along the river shores were destroyed by the great hurricane of that year.

Daddy was the eldest in his family. His siblings were Corie, Ben, and

Lucy.

Corie (Cornelia Carter H.) was unfortunately stricken with polio encephalitis when she was nine or ten years old. She suffered no paralysis of her limbs, but the high fever caused her to have some mental damage. She had a phenomenal memory but it seemed that her emotional development had been stunted and she was never able to function as a completely normal person. Nanee's life was devoted to attending to Corie with the utmost patience and Christian devotion. Corie had been named for "Antie" (Corie C. Chilton), who had reared Nanee.

Ben (Benjamin Newton H.) attended both Fork Union Academy, in Orange County, and William and Mary College, as my dad had done. In those days many young men in Lancaster County attended both of those schools. Later Ben was postmaster at White Stone until he served in the U.S. Army postal department in France during World War II. When he returned from the war my dad took him into his insurance business in Kilmarnock. Ben married Nancy Crawford, whose family moved from Richmond to White Stone in the late 1930s.

Lucy (Lucy Elizabeth H.) was Dad's younger sister. She was said to be a very frail young child who was saved by eating "Mellin's Food," a commercial baby food of that time. The odd thing about this was that the baby who was pictured on the Mellin's Food container was John Taylor Green of Natchez, Mississippi, whom Lucy later met and married. They met during World War II, while she was teaching school in Hampton and he was serving as a U. S. Naval Officer in Hampton Roads and on the Chesapeake Bay for practice maneuvers. Lucy had attended the State Teachers College at Harrisonburg (now James Madison University). I called Lucy "Suta" for many years, and many people said that we looked alike. When I was very young this always bothered me and I would immediately reply, "I look like myself." Well—so much for my independent nature! Nevertheless, I grew up feeling a close kindred spirit with Suta. She was always very good to me. When she and John lived in Natchez, my husband, Irwin Clark, and I had many wonderful visits with them there in that grand old Southern town. Irwin and John were very much alike in many ways. Though we were much younger than Lucy and John we were very compatible. Both fellows were very Southern and Lucy and I shared many of the same interests.

The Farm

At Waterview Farm, the business of running the farm was mainly done by my grandmother, Nanee, since grandfather was usually on a business trip out of the county. There was a tenant farm family living there and also three hired men who were the farm workers. The head man and his family lived in the tenant house across the cove from the main house. They had come from King George County and were an interesting mix of American Indian, black, and white ancestry. His name was Richard and he had a large family of nine children—eight boys and one little girl. His wife, "Queenie," worked in the house helping Nanee. Queenie was quite a bossy character who seemed capable of handling anything and everything, no matter what the task or situation. Their oldest son's name was "George" and another was named "Benjamin Franklin." Since their family name was "Washington," we could say that they were surely patriots. Upon reflection, the family might have been descended from workers on the Washingtons' farm at Pope's Creek in Westmoreland County where our president, George, was born. It's close to King George County. In colonial times, often workers took the name of the family for whom they worked.

Waterview Farm was not a large farming operation. The acres of wheat, barley, soybeans, and corn were grown on land near the house and in fields that extended for about a distance of two miles on one side of the road over to the creek shore. I have no idea of the acreage this involved.

Many Sundays after the midday dinner I walked with my dad when he went to "check on the lower fields." A large field of tomatoes—or soybeans in alternating years—grew on five or six acres fronting the house out to the roadside.

When Father was living, following dessert after the midday Sunday dinner he would push his chair back from the table to light up his cigar. He loved discussing politics and a heated political argument usually developed with his two adult sons: my "Daddy Charlie" and Uncle Ben, who was a bachelor at the time. The ladies at the table never entered into these forays. As the men's voices escalated to a high pitch, I quietly crept away from the table and hid under the big knee-hole desk in the sitting room. There I found refuge from all of the "fussing"—I thought—and the hated smell of Father's cigar smoke. I know that his cigar kept me from loving him as I might have. The adults thought that he was quite a fine Victorian gentleman.

I was the only grandchild of the family in the years before the farm was sold. On those Sundays at Waterview I liked to go into the parlor, alone, and try to play the old flat-top, four-legged Chickering piano that was badly in need of tuning. I'm sure it had not been played for many years, as there were certainly no pianists in my dad's family at the time. There were a few sheets of old piano music still resting on top of the piano and one of the songs was entitled "In the Gloaming." That odd title still rings a bell in my memory. It was surely a leftover from Victorian days.

Also in the parlor, there was a fine china figurine sitting on the mantelshelf above the fireplace. The china figures standing together on its base were a young peasant boy and girl. The barefoot young boy wore breeches rolled to his knees, had a companion dog at his side, and carried a fishing pole slung over his shoulder. The girl was dressed in an ankle length full skirt with a pretty bodice laced up and worn over her blouse. One of her hands was outstretched bearing grain to feed a pair of chickens down beside her bare feet. The two figures were dressed in pastel outfits and had delicate chiseled facial features. I thought that they were beautiful. Nanee understood how much I loved this figurine, so she would take the china piece down from its perch on the mantel and place it on the parlor rug for me to lie and scrutinize—up close, but not to touch. Later in my life I credited this early "examining" as an exercise that helped to develop in me an appreciation for detail and beauty. Well, it might've been an early beginning for my enjoyment of such things that came along in my adult life. Some of the family thought that Nanee was "spoiling" me when she removed the figurine from the mantel for my pleasure. She was always a dear and wonderful person and I believe that there was some wisdom in her allowing me to have this kind of aesthetic experience. She definitely earned my love when I was very young.

Private telephone lines were generally unavailable in rural areas such as Antipoison Neck. A "party line" was an arrangement of two or three telephones (parties) that were all connected on one line. Each phone on the line was assigned a number of phone rings (i.e., one or two rings) for its own call. The user answered the call upon hearing the number of rings assigned to its phone. It was easy to overhear conversations on the party line. The rude listener could simply place the phone receiver to the ear and remain mute while listening to another person's phone conversation. I learned this devilish trick when I was quite young. It embarrassed me to be caught in my mischief.

In the wintertime, I often had a great time entertaining myself by sneaking into the cold, empty dining room whenever the phone rang. It was lodged on the wall in that room, centrally located in the big old house. I loved to listen to conversations of people who were talking at the other end of the "party line." Because doors were closed in all of the unheated rooms I could secretly enjoy this private amusement. Nanee sometimes caught me thus engaged and, with a slight smile and a twinkle in her eye, she admonished me gently with "you little scamp."

One cool autumn day Daddy took me with him to sit on the dock at the edge of the creek and learn to eat oysters. He shucked them, dipped them one-by-one into a cup of vinegar and served each one to me after placing it on the top of a big soda cracker. I hesitated to agree that the bivalves tasted good, but I left the dock chatting agreeably with him about this newly discovered edible. I wanted to please him. My dad was determined that his daughter must love to eat oysters. After all, living in our "oyster world" required it.

Another time down at the creekside was the day when my "at-home" playmate, Jackie Hughes, went with me to Waterview for a day visit. We tramped in the marsh grass and gathered periwinkle shells. These tiny green snail-like creatures could be found attached to the base of most of the marsh grasses. We had been told to talk to a periwinkle and coach him to come out of his shell by holding one in our hand and slowly chanting, in a low monotonous tone, this little ditty:

Periwinkle, Periwinkle
Come out your shell,
Don't, I'll beat you cold
As a fire coal, fire coal.

And finally, with plenty of repeated chants, it worked. It really did. At least, we thought that it was the chanting that did it.

That same day Nanee made a treat for us to take home—homemade doughnuts. We rode home sitting on the back seat of my parents' car and ate every doughnut in each of our bags before reaching home—a distance of about ten miles. Yum! We hastily gulped down those sugary morsels with zest. We country kids knew nothing of city treats like doughnuts. It was surely a scrumptious way to end our day. But we never really understood why the periwinkles that we were carrying home with us, inside of the pockets of Jackie's leather aviator jacket, had crawled out of their shells. We hadn't told them to do THAT.

Daddy and I hiked the long trek to Clark Point from the house each December to get our cedar Christmas tree and drag it back to the house. Somehow it was always an exciting and wonderful outing, no matter how far the distance seemed on foot. At other times I went with him into the woods to go squirrel hunting across the road from the farm. He never got off a shot when I was in tow, but I had served as his partner and it was a great hunting adventure for me. He didn't have a son, so I was serving as one instead.

Down at the barn I liked to watch the hired men slopping the pigs, harnessing horses, or driving the cows and horses to the water trough. I always kept myself at a good distance from all of this action. I best liked the kittens at the barn. I could never quite get over the sight of the horses' green teeth that were revealed when they drank at the trough. It made me shudder to see that grimy and disgusting sight. I thought it was repulsive.

Once Daddy decided that I should learn to ride horses, so he saw to it that I had a new pair of jodhpurs that we ordered from the Sears, Roebuck and Co. catalog. Sears and Roebuck, as we called it, was known to lots of country folks in the thirties as "the wish book." I'm sure that I must have been a great disappointment to my dad when the day came for my first lesson because, just as I settled on the saddle, a huge horsefly lit on the horse's rear end. That horse swished his tail, immediately began to shimmy and neigh, then took off galloping, with me on his back, almost to the end of the long lane. Daddy and Richard Washington had to rescue me. That was my last horseback ride. The event had frightened me to death. I was cured forever of any love of horses which might have developed.

There was a footbridge across the marsh where the cove ended in front of the fenced yard on the front side of the house. Often I went with my aunt, Corie, across the bridge to feed the turkeys that were kept in an area of the big field on the other side of the marsh. We also scouted around the shoreline of the cove in search of muscadine grapes. This was always a tiresome excursion for me. I really wasn't very enthusiastic about that outing. There were brambles everywhere, but Corie was never daunted by the task and always came home proud of all the fine muscadines that we had managed to collect.

The main house at Waterview was set well back from the waters of Antipoison Creek with a broad lawn that extended out to the creek. There was an ancient, fenced-in family burial plot at one side of the lawn. All of the grave markers there had disappeared, but it was the resting place of our early family members.

Waterview Farm, 1930s photo

Waterview was a three-story, white frame house that originally had no front porches or dormers. The early part of the house was built in the late 1780s. A pair of dormer windows and front porches, upper and lower, had been added in the late 1800's. At the rear of the house, in about 1905, my grandfather ("Father") had made an addition for the dining room with a large bedroom and bathroom space above it. He also added the large screened porch outside of the parlor, on the creekside of the house. The old dairy and smokehouse still stood within the fenced yard. The original outside kitchen building had been brought up to the main house at the same time and was attached to the house with an entryway. I remember the tiny dark stairway that led up to the cook's room of early times. It was above the original kitchen but was no longer in use.

Nanee had many pretty flowerbeds inside the pale fencing that surrounded the yard. Her peonies, iris, and hydrangeas were especially memorable to me. Outside the yard the new garage housed two Hudson Terraplane automobiles that were exactly alike. One was kept stored with its wheels set up on blocks. I never understood this. Maybe Father kept a spare in case one car was occasionally out of commission. No one ever explained about the second identical car.

The house was tall, so it was easy to imagine my grandmother's horror when, one time, she found her young son, Ben, walking around the edge of the rooftop. Another of her amusing "little boy stories" was about my dad. She said that the family awoke one Christmas morning to find that my "Daddy Charlie," then a young lad, had taken the Christmas tree down and was dragging it outside into the yard. Times really don't change things a lot: "Boys Will Be Boys!"

In the 1930s there was no central heat in the house at the farm and wood burning stoves were used in each room. All of the fireplaces had been sealed to accommodate the stoves. It was a cold walk between rooms where the stoves were not in use. Also, Aladdin oil lamps were the best lamp light after the metal table oil lamps, which had been used earlier. Both produced light by burning a wick set down into a lamp bowl that was filled with oil. Some of the gaslight fixtures of former times were still in place on walls in a few of the rooms, but were no longer functional. Antipoison Neck didn't get electricity until the late nineteen thirties. The old wooden ice box, which had served as refrigeration for food, still stood in the entryway between the dining room and kitchen. A large electric Kelvinator refrigerator had replaced use of the ice box by this point in time.

Nanee's big 1860's tester bed from Ditchley had been her mother's bed. That bed always fascinated me and I loved the adventure of sleeping in it, even though the mattress was uncomfortably firm. A pair of bronze statues of "Don Juan" and "Don Cezar" were on the mantel in the sitting room. They were positioned there in gallant poses, guarding the old black metal pillar clock that stood between them. Those gentlemen were a curiosity to me. Whenever I sat on Nanee's lap I always gazed at them intently while the clock chimed the hour in sharp tingling dins.

Often in the wintertime our family stayed at the farm for Sunday night supper. After eating we sat in the sitting room for me to listen to the Charlie McCarthy radio program and *The Jack Benny Program*, which I loved. When the programs ended I lay there on the sofa with Nanee rubbing my foot and the faint hum of the adults' conversation lulled me into a sound sleep. Then my parents could pick me up in their arms and carry me home while I dozed in contentment.

On warm summer evenings the family gathered on the screened porch at the back of the house. There in the darkness we listened to the chorus of katydids chanting and hawking their "cha-cha" calls in waves of competition, high in the nearby oak trees. The treat of the evening was when the homemade peach ice cream was served. We all settled in contentment after enjoying the mellow taste of this wonderful icy dish, hand churned by my dad and fresh from the wooden ice cream freezer. No place in my early life holds a sweeter memory than those enchanted porch times, surrounded by the warmth of all of the family.

My grandfather died in 1937. Ben was drafted into the Army during World War II and my parents were living in Kilmarnock. Due to his age, Daddy had narrowly missed the draft and was working to build his insurance business while running the farm and attending to Nanee and Corie there. In 1946, after the war had ended, both Daddy and Ben

Daddy and me on the porch at Waterview, 1944.

were living in Kilmarnock so Waterview was sold out of the family. This was done in order to move Nanee and Corie to Kilmarnock where Nanee could be closer to her sons in her advancing years, which would make life simpler for all.

My dad reserved the tenant house across the cove and remodeled it into a summer cottage. We called it "Breezy Cove" and spent some wonderful summers there.

IV

Right Around Home

Kilmarnock

The town of my birth was where I grew up and enjoyed a very happy childhood during the thirties and forties. The town was first known as "The Crossroads," then became "Steptoe's Ordinary," and finally was named "Kilmarnock." It became incorporated in 1930, the year when I was born.

My family's first home on Irvington Road.

On Irvington Road

O ur house stood on Irvington Road, a few blocks down from Main Street and close to the old high school. When I was a very young child I loved for Mother to rock me in the wicker rocking chair that was in our den by the window that faced "uptown." As she rocked me she sang this little song:

> I had a little pony – his name was "Dapple Grey"
> I lent him to a lady
> To ride a mile away –
> She whipped him; she lashed him;
> She drove him through the mire –
> I would not lend my pony now
> For all that lady's hire.

I never knew why the song was so appealing to me, but undoubtedly, it was the sound of her soothing soft voice as she sang and rocked me in that chair.

The stillness of the street was interrupted early each morning by the sound of milk bottles being delivered to our front doorstep by the Bunker Hill Dairy that was operated by one of my dad's cousins, Flexmer Chase.

On early Sunday mornings, along with the milk delivery came the Sunday funnies. I ran eagerly downstairs to get the newspaper and dash back to jump into bed between my parents for Daddy to read the funny papers to me. The best of all was "Dick Tracy," I thought. But I also liked "Blondie" and "Maggie and Jiggs." Dagwood and Mrs. Plushbottom were two of my favorite characters. "Popeye" and "Gasoline Alley" were also high up on my list.

Many times, very early on those Sunday mornings, my dad got a call from Phil Emery, who yelled to him from under my parents' upstairs bedroom window until Daddy finally responded. Phil's plea was always the same: "Cap'n Cholli, pleez let me have a quatta—I reely needs it, suh." That "reel" need for a quarter was, of course, to buy another bottle of wine—the 1930's price of his wine. Phil was an engaging and respectful gray-haired black fellow, a very gentlemanly type, except for his habitual dependence on wine. He was very proud of his gold front tooth that he loved to show to everyone. But it was sad to see him staggering along the street when he was drunk. Daddy certainly should have refused to help Phil get more wine. He probably felt sorry for him, as well as wanting to continue his Sunday morning sleep. After all, that was supposed to be the "day of rest."

During the daytime and on many evenings we could hear the trumpet practice of our next-door neighbor, "Junior" Harvey. In warm weather the young fellow sat beside an open window, on the side of his house that was next to ours, and blew the loud notes that drifted over into our house. It seemed as though his practice sessions would never end. The shrill discordant stops and starts of the repetition pierced our ears and the monotony of his diligence annoyed us until we became frazzled with impatience. However, Junior's determination earned him the reward of becoming an accomplished trumpeter, though he never became any competition for Harry James. As he matured, Junior later formed a local band of his own. Little did I realize that I would be dancing to his horn-playing when I attended Beach dances when I began dating.

Miss Janie Kenner, usually called, "Ant Janie," was a curious sight whenever she plodded, afoot, past our house, heading uptown. She was a tall, thin black lady who was said to be of part Indian blood. Her unruffled nature made her a well-liked and well-known personality. She was always dressed in a long, full skirt that touched the top of the boots that she always wore. Her head was bound by a turban headdress, and long strands of beads swung low as they dangled around her neck. She usually carried a very large bag at her side, probably for shopping. We anxiously peered, straining to catch sight of her gold tooth. It shone brightly whenever she grinned while she puffed on the corncob pipe that was clenched between her teeth. All of us kids rushed to see her whenever we heard, "Ant Janie's coming."

In the thirties and forties, Ira Grimes was the fish man who came infrequently in the summertime selling fish that were fresh from the docks at the river. He hawked his "fish man" call up and down the streets all over town while he continued honking on the truck's horn. The fish were sold from the back of his ice-filled truck that left a trail of melting ice as it rumbled along the streets. He stopped to park in front of each home where a lady came out bearing a large pan for her purchases. Ira Grimes was something

Moorman home (left) and McKenney home (right), on Irvington Road, across from our house.

of a legend in town. He was a good-natured and jolly black man. People always greeted him with enthusiasm. When he talked—explaining the fish and the prices—his chubby body rocked back and forth and he jiggled up and down on his feet, shaking his head in a bobbing motion. He was often heard to emphatically proclaim, "Yes indeedy ma'm, they sho' is fresh today."

Louise and Mac (Earnest) McKenney lived across the street from us. We could see them working together in their yard in the late afternoon of each and every day. They never missed. They diligently tended their many shrubs and garden plants, keeping all in perfect horticultural order. They were real garden lovers. Their boxwood-lined front sidewalk was the centerpiece of their street-side front yard. It was flanked on either side by a collection of beautiful flowering shrubs. Their yard was the showplace of the neighborhood.

Play Days

My first playmate was Jackie Hughes. His dad owned and operated the Nehi Bottling Co. uptown on East Church Street. I was six

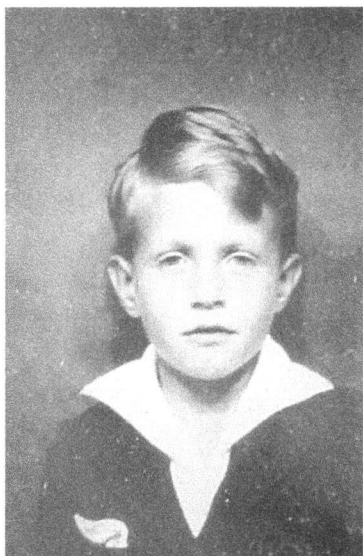

Jackie Hughes. *Photo courtesy of his daughter, Danise.*

months older than Jackie, to the day. He lived down on Second Avenue, around the corner from Irvington Road, not far from my home. At the end of the avenue the sidewalk turned left onto the next street (later to become Claybrook Avenue) and there was a ball diamond in the field nearby. At the corner was a large low spot that usually flooded and filled up when there were heavy rains.

One cold winter day when Jackie and I were riding our tricycles, he was tearing full-steam ahead of me, racing into the huge mud hole at the corner. We were both dressed in our heavy woolen snowsuits that nearly all children wore in the thirties. Being "older and wiser," I kept yelling to him, giving him warnings about getting stuck in that mud hole. But he defied my bossing by pedaling even harder until he'd reached the deepest part of the muddy pool where his race came to a dead end. He was firmly stuck there. He toppled over into the water and that was when The Great War erupted between us. I chided him for being dumb. Drenched in that heavy snowsuit he became a furious wet dragon, floundering in the middle of a sea of brown water that was ankle deep. We ended the war by screaming and crying, then running home to our mommas, cold and shivering in our rage.

Forever afterward both of us remembered the incident. We were still laughing together about "The Great Mudhole War" up until his untimely death, some seventy-three years later, in 2007.

In those early days Jackie and I played such games as Cowboys and Indians; made roads in the sand for our toy cars; flew kites that we sometimes made from newspapers—and which never managed to lift into the air; played a game we called "Tommy Can't Find Me" that was simply hiding from his younger brother; and at Halloween, did the "Tic-Tac" trick on his house. This was a classic Halloween prank. The trick called for quietly inserting a long nail up under the clapboard siding of his parents' house. Then we attached a long length of twine to the nail and unrolled it to a distance in the yard where we could hide and yet see into the house. There we watched for his dad's reaction as we rubbed a piece of rosin over the string. We had purchased it at the drugstore for our prank. This action was supposed to cause a noise inside the house that sounded like the board siding was being ripped from the walls. It must have caused some degree of the desired effect for I remember how excited we became when we saw his dad rise up from his chair to look out of the window. So naturally we promptly ran from the yard, afraid of being caught in our mischief.

The "Jackie days" ended for me when the neighborhood girls on Irvington Road came of age. That was when I deserted Jackie to play "girl stuff."

Girl playtime was very serious business. It was almost a daily routine of highly organized play that we girls carefully planned. Upsetting interruptions were marked only by rainy days or freezing temperatures. Our great days of open-air play lasted most of the entire year, and continued for about three years.

The group of girls in our wonderful world of play days included Rebecca Lou Dixon, Frances Moorman, her sister, Dixie, who was a little younger than the rest of us, so she usually wasn't fully active in our play routine, Mary Frances Harvey, and the Allen sisters, Jane and Marion.

Frances and Dixie's dad was Dr. E. R. Moorman, who had come to the county to establish a medical practice in town. Dr. Moorman built his home/office diagonally across the street from our house. Frances's "Grandad," who lived with them, built a log cabin playhouse for us in the woods behind their home. It still stands today, a ghostly reminder

1937 Playmates: Me with Rebecca Lou Dixon and Frances Moorman.

of the happy days of our childhood. He created a large play area of high-wire fencing around it for us girls. Each day we could hardly wait to "get over to the log cabin" for the day's playtime. We even had a special kind of yodel, or "call," to come to play, whenever we wanted to communicate. From our homes we gave the "aye-awr-eeet" call, loudly sounding out the throaty howl. It was our coded message meaning: "I'm ready—are you ready?" Our call alerted the entire neighborhood that our gang of girls was in its play-action mode. On the quiet street our calls could easily be heard up and down Irvington Road and for several blocks away.

The log cabin playhouse, a relic in 2009.

Along with the cabin, their grandad had contrived a merry-go-round/see-saw from the trunk of a tall old pine tree. He also made two handmade sets of swings for our fun times. For the merry-go-round, Grandad had cut a large pine tree and mounted it horizontally across a big tree stump. Evidently the stump had some sort of metal pole fixed in its center to serve as an axis. Then the pole was projected up through a hole that was at a point midway along the log. The result was amazing. We could ride at each end of the log where he had constructed two handlebars for us to hold onto, in order for two girls to ride on each end of the log, so that four of us could ride at once. We could bounce up and down for a see-saw motion, but for merry-go-round rides, one or two of us would have to push the log to make it go around. We ran and pushed until the rides became a dizzying whirl. There were often arguments among us as to who was to push and who would get to ride. These were "whirl-away" days and no modern contraption could produce more fun than Grandad's innovation had done for us.

There were also cages where rabbits were kept in the play yard, as well as a few bantam chickens. It was truly a child's paradise. Picnics, hide 'n' seek games and a Halloween spook house were all part of the scene.

Choices of what to play and who was to be "it" for a game of hide 'n' seek on a given day were always the first order of each play-day planning agenda. Occasionally the choices provoked some arguments. Many times Mary Frances would run home to "tell my mama" when she didn't win the choice of play for the day. We were heartless by not letting her win more often than we did: she was a little younger than the rest of us. Being the only girl in her family of brothers, undoubtedly she was spoiled at home.

Playing dolls under the McKenney garden arbor: Rebecca Lou, Frances M., my cousin Gerry, and me.

Her mother called her "my little gull."

Louise McKenney, who lived across the street from us, had no children of her own, but was Rebecca Lou's aunt. Rebecca Lou spent each full day with Louise and then went to her home, further down the street, to spend the nights with her family. It was in Louise's magical flower garden behind the house that we played "weddings" under her rose arbor. We dressed up in clothes that we found in her attic, including a collection of 1920s flapper-style dresses. We also found several old German china dolls that we used along with our own dolls when we played doll-babies under the shade of the big umbrella tree in her backyard. Louise enjoyed all of us. She once read *Miss Minerva and William Green Hill* to us while we sat on her porch in the afternoons, and several times, at night, she had us come to see the blooming of her prized nightblooming cereus plant. She played the piano for us to sing together. I especially remember when we gathered around her piano and sang "Yankee Doodle Dandy" after we'd seen the James Cagney movie uptown at the Fairfax.

Mrs. Cutler lived next door to the Moormans, in the big Victorian house (now Ross's Rings and Things) where there were several large old shade trees in the yard. She was a very dear little lady who had a tiny, cheerful voice. She often came out into the shady yard, huffing and puffing, to serve us cookies and lemonade. From her open kitchen door the aroma of tantalizing goodies was always in the air. It was her usual custom to bake a small birthday cake for any child in her Methodist Sunday school class who was having a birthday. Often, in her high-pitched little voice, she would ask us, "Now what are you girls playing today?" We all loved Mrs. Cutler.

Back at my home across the street, my mother also had a nice flower garden, though not as extensive as the McKenney one. Mother was not the avid gardener that Louise McKenney was, so she often had Willie Grimes come and help with the gardening tasks. He was known and respected in town for his gardening expertise. We also had "weddings" in Mother's garden. We wore my mother's discarded evening dresses and used her old sheer curtains for wedding veils. In our double-car garage we put on shows and strung a line of more curtains for the stage. I was always the director of our productions because I was the oldest in the group of girls. We were strongly influenced by the movies that we regularly attended at the Fairfax. Imitation was always our model for action—with some innovation guiding our themes. I remember one of our shows that included part of a song from a movie that we had seen starring Wallace Beery and Marjorie Main. We sang and loudly shouted "ta-ra-ra Boom-de-ay" as we performed our chorus line kicks to the tune.

We played "tea parties" in my small playhouse at the back of our garage, using my set of Blue Willow doll china. Once we had a band, using the toy instruments that Santa had brought to me at Christmas. When we had a birthday, all of our birthday parties were standard events with the classic ice cream and cake menu and the Pin-the-Tail-on-the-Donkey game. It never varied. The birthday presents were the highlight of the parties. We always sat around in a circle while the birthday child unwrapped each gift. We all thought that this was the most exciting part of the party and couldn't wait for the unwrapping to begin.

The joys of those early playtimes could hardly be matched anywhere else in the world. Money was never a necessity for the kind of great fun that we had.

Whenever I was alone I often became fully immersed in playing paper dolls. I spent hours with both the "Gone With the Wind" and "Ziegfield Girl" paper dolls. They were the two big movies of the era and their costumes seemed gorgeous and dazzling to me.

One summer in the early forties my mother allowed me to keep my paper dollies lined up for weeks on every step of our staircase at home. I spent nearly that entire summer drawing, designing, and coloring clothes for each of the Ziegfield paper doll stars: Hedy Lamarr, Lana Turner, Veronica Lake, Judy Garland, Georgia Carroll, Carmen Miranda, and the rest. What a mess I did make with it all spread out on our living room floor, but somehow Mother patiently allowed me to have that creative fun time. I'm sure that she must've been glad when I finally tired of it and put away all of my litter.

School Days

The old schoolhouse (Kilmarnock High School), 1930s. *Photo courtesy of Kilmarnock Museum.*

The large white frame schoolhouse stood diagonally across the street from my home on Irvington Road. Seven elementary grades and four years of high school were all together in the building. The old metal school bell could be heard all over town each time it rang for classes to change or when the school day began or ended.

All of the students were white children from Kilmarnock, the Taylor's Creek, Fleet's Bay Neck and Black Stump areas. Other schools of the county were in White Stone, Irvington, Weems, Lively, and the Mollusk area. The old Lancaster School had been closed for many years. Schools for black children were located outside of Kilmarnock, near White Stone, and in the Upper Lancaster area.

Two large classrooms were downstairs in our school. The first grade and a section of second grade occupied one room. Both second and third grades were together in the other room. Two classrooms were upstairs at the front of the building: one for the fourth and fifth grades and one for the sixth and seventh grades. The four years of high school occupied four rooms at the rear of the building. All of this was, no doubt, an inadequately cozy arrangement. A large auditorium was downstairs at the rear of the building, where certain activities were held. These were primarily chapel services, held on Friday mornings; school plays; and the Christmas "White Gift Service." The latter functioned as an outreach activity to help the needy people of the area. Children brought cans of food, which they presented, wrapped in white, as offerings of charity. This was usually a solemn service of candlelight, prayers, and hymn singing. The Friday morning chapel services were always conducted by visiting community church ministers, usually Baptist or Methodist.

Each class day began with the student body reciting the Pledge of Allegiance to the Flag—either outside on the school grounds where "Old Glory" was raised or inside of our classrooms in wet weather. A student safety patrolman was honored with the job of hoisting the flag up on the flagpole outside. The safety patrol was the group of responsible high school boys who performed duties of street safety for children leaving the school grounds at the end of the day, as well as supervising them as they boarded or got off of school buses. Safety patrol members were chosen by the faculty.

At this point in time, I hurried home every afternoon to hear my favorite serials on the radio. Each one lasted fifteen minutes and the programs I liked were "Pepper Young's Family," "Ma Perkins," and "Stella Dallas." I sat beside a big window in our den and, while listening to the shows, I crunched my standard afternoon snack of honey graham crackers and sipped ginger ale from my blue glass Shirley Temple mug. By five o'clock I rushed back to crouch beside our Zenith radio that stood on the floor in our living room. I tuned in to hear "Captain Midnight" and "Jack Armstrong, the All-American Boy." Those adventure stories excited my imagination. Jackie and I loved these two programs and we both ordered the Captain Midnight secret code badges when we were in third grade. Wearing them always made us feel important.

The old school had no central heat and each room was heated by a large wood-burning stove. A kettle of water was kept boiling on top of the stove, giving off steam to humidify the stuffy, offensive air in the room. Aromas of wet feet were noticeably acute—along with other pungent odors—so it was no wonder that during the day the teacher often opened the window for an invigorating breath of fresh air. A ventilating system was unheard of in the old building.

Pupils were required to "raise your hand to be excused." This meant a trip outside to the "johnny house," located at the back of the schoolyard. But usually recess time was when we stood in line outside of the privy for our turn inside of the three-holer. We shivered and giggled as we accepted the limitations of luxury afforded by this standard kind of necessary facility at the time.

The games we played at recess were mainly dodge ball; hop scotch; or jump rope. The girls played bob jacks with their best friends and boys played marbles with their buddies. By the time we reached fourth grade we played some softball, which I hated. There were three ball fields on the school grounds. Baseball was always a big thing for the school children.

I started first grade at age seven because my birthday came too late in the summer for me to begin school when I was six. There was no kindergarten in the school system, nor at any of the area churches at the time. We had no eighth grade in those days either, so children went directly from seventh grade into high school.

My first grade teacher, Miss Elenora Haynie, was adored by all of her students. Her loving and gentle manner remained forever fixed in the minds of everyone who had been in her classroom. "Nona" never forgot the children she taught. She loved them all and managed to remember them in special ways as they grew older. She remained unmarried for most of her life and was finally married—late in life— to Mr. Henderson Porter, an old bachelor gentleman. They went to live at his home on "Porter's Hill," just outside of town, where we all went sleigh riding on that wonderful hill behind his house.

Mr. Henri B. Chase was principal of the school. His office was on the second floor, just above the front entrance of the school. Sometimes one of the boys would be sent to the principal's

My first-grade picture, with the important hair bow of each day, 1937.

office as the strongest form of punishment when disciplinary action was required. A teacher's threat of "I'm going to send you to Mr. Chase's office!" was usually effective and the student's behavior was promptly held in check. However, actually being sent to the office was looked upon, by innocent observers, as an embarrassment for the guilty party. Mr. Chase must have given powerful and emphatic talks to his guilty subjects for we never heard of any corporal punishment being used and the offender's bad behavior was immediately squelched following the visit.

The fourth grade classroom was at the front of the building, adjacent to his office. The teacher was Miss Nellie Gordon Chase, his sister. Each room had a cloakroom, where coats and lunch boxes were kept as well as the firewood for burning in the schoolroom stove.

A memorable day for all of us, when I was in fourth grade, was the day when Miss Chase delivered one of her strong disciplinary punishments to our entire class. Her niece, Jeanne Blake, my classmate and best friend, had stored her lunch box, along with all of the others, on the cloakroom shelf above our coats. Miss Chase left the classroom for a few minutes to speak to Mr. Chase. In that brief time one of the boys discovered Jeanne's lunchbox with milk pouring outside from the broken thermos bottle inside of it. This fellow came out of the cloak room, held the leaking lunch box high while he gleefully made jokes about it, causing the whole class to break into a great roar of laughter.

At this high point in the drama Miss Chase suddenly opened the classroom door. She came in and a red-faced rage immediately surged over her as she confronted the riotous giggles that had engulfed all of us trapped little darlings. Needless to say, a pall of heavy silence befell our group. We knew that we had been caught and that severe punishment loomed ahead for all of us. And we were RIGHT. She delivered an unforgettable lesson. The entire class was kept after school and made to write, one hundred times, this sentence: "I will not laugh at other people's mistakes or misfortunes." It was a good lesson, to be sure, but a long sentence for ten year-olds to write so many times. We were not allowed to begin the writing until the three-o'clock bell rang to end the school day. It seemed that I finally got home around four-thirty in the afternoon. I could walk the short distance to my home, but I have no idea what the bus riders did to get to their homes on that awful day.

Also while I was in fourth grade, a sad day for me was when my dog, "Sport"—actually Daddy's bird-hunting dog, a setter—had to be put to sleep. Sport was infected by distemper disease, which, at the time, affected many dogs. The preventive vaccination for distemper had not then been developed. I had been told that the veterinarian would come in the morning to perform the terrible deed. Unfortunately, I stood and looked out of the upstairs classroom window. From afar I could see the dreaded scene taking place across the street in the yard at my home. Someone should have kept me away from the window. It was my first tough loss in life.

Moving day for the school also happened when I was in fourth grade. This was certainly a momentous event in our school's history.

The new brick school building was located down the dirt road—now School Street—a distance of approximately three city blocks. Each of us walked the distance lugging our own desk. Naturally many starts and stops were made on this full school-day excursion. Much good-humored excitement prevailed. The daunting task of such labor didn't begin to phase us. After all, we were children of the Great Depression and had never been used to luxury. This day was a perfect lark for us. The shiny new school, outfitted with radiator central heat and inside toilets, was a dream come true. Now the outdoor privy, with the shivering wait in long lines, was to be a welcomed part of the past.

The new school (Kilmarnock High School).

Uptown

Often after school I went uptown to visit Jeanne, whose home was on Main Street, where the Bank of Lancaster now stands (2009). We did a lot of roller skating and sometimes skated over to the East Coast Utilities office and rolled on into the alley where the telephone office was located at the rear of the building. We could skate right up to the door window there and observe the ladies when they were operating the two switchboards. This always fascinated us. We got a chuckle when we watched the plump young operator who chewed and popped gum while she answered and transferred calls. We thought she was very clever the way she could talk

Fairfax Theatre, 1929. *Photo courtesy of Kilmarnock Museum.*

and pop chewing gum, all the while operating her switchboard. It was a great amusement for us.

The Fairfax Theatre was our biggest touch with the outside world. Each week the feature picture changed three times. Movies were only shown at nighttime. There were no matinees. The three shows were on Monday-Tuesday; Wednesday-Thursday; and Friday-Saturday. There were no Sunday movies until the late 1940s. Wednesday night was Bank Night with an admission ticket drawing for a cash prize of $25.00, or a $25.00 War Bond during World War II. These drawings lasted only a few years. They were incentives to lure people to the midweek movie attraction. Admission prices for tickets went up from fifteen cents to twenty-five cents, to thirty-five cents and fifty cents and higher in the early nineteen fifties.

In the thirties, we kids regularly attended the Western or cowboy movies on Friday nights. When we saw cowboy movies at the Fairfax, it was always easy to recognize our hero as the good guy amidst the struggle between good and bad guys. He rode on a white horse, wore a big white hat and was dressed in white. Conversely, the villain was garbed in black and rode a dark horse. The lesson of good versus evil was easy for us

Hazel Building with upstairs Opera House, site of dance revues. Main Street, Kilmarnock, 1930s. *Photo courtesy of Kilmarnock Museum.*

to understand and we left the movie meaning to use it in our own real-life story. After all, the good guys always won!

Two of those hero-stars that I especially liked were Tex Ritter and Roy Rogers. But Gene Autry was my real favorite, with his guitar-playing and singing. I never missed a Gene Autry movie when it came to town.

Attending the Saturday night movie was always taboo because it was the night when the town was filled with crowds of people. This was the big grocery shopping night of the week for many throughout the countryside. It was also a social outing for these people and sometimes things could get rough. An occasional fight developed among excessive drinkers, even though there was no liquor store in town. Whiskey and also "moonshine" from unknown sources seemed readily available. It served to promote some wild behavior and a lot of "whooping it up" along the sidewalks of Main Street, uptown. By eleven o'clock the Saturday night throng disappeared and the town "shut down," returning to its usual mode of tranquility.

Fairfax Theatre opened in 1927. It was established by my grandmother's (Nanee's) brother, Rawleigh D. Carter, who became the town's first mayor in 1930. He and his wife, Mary Chase Carter, operated the theater until his death in 1933. "Ant Mary," as I called her, continued to operate the Fairfax for many years thereafter, along with her sister-in-law, Carrie Kamps Chase, who was always a presence at the ticket sale window.

When it opened, the theater had an exterior Spanish architectural style of the California 1920s period. That was where moving pictures had been developed and were being produced. This style of architecture, to me, has always seemed oddly in conflict with the theater's colonial name of "Fairfax." That name had obviously originated with the Colonial Virginia historical figure, Lord Fairfax. His proprietary agent had been Robert "King" Carter, whose home and seat of operations were here in Lancaster

County, at Weems. The California architecture reflected the new moving-picture era that had begun.

The Fairfax was surely a modern innovation on the Northern Neck. It remained the only movie theater on the lower Neck until after World War II when the Lee Theatre opened at White Stone and operated for several years. Briefly during those same years, Pitts Drive-In movie operated at the north end of Kilmarnock, as well as the theater in Reedville and one in Callao. But no other theater, for miles around, was a more vibrant entertainment center for twelve months of the year than the Fairfax Theatre.

In 1935, the Firemen's Carnival began its traditional nighttime summertime event. It operated to benefit the all-volunteer fire department. The event was first held on Waverly Avenue, next to the Edmond's home (formerly Lewson Chase's Kilmarnock Seminary). It then continued, for many years, on Irvington Road, where the present day Tri-Star Super Market is located. Finally the carnival was moved to its current site at the top of the hill on Waverly Avenue.

Crowds of people, primarily from Lancaster and Northumberland counties, met for years during each night of the carnival to see old friends and enjoy the event with its tradition of family fun in a safe environment. Few incidents of rowdiness marked the event and crime was a non-factor. As time passed, young children matured and returned later, as adults, to bring their offspring back to enjoy their childhood haunt of fun and frolic. In later years people began to come from afar for a summer evening of fun and reunions.

For most of the carnival years the merry-go-round, swings, and Ferris wheel dominated the scene as the major rides. As time passed new rides and games were introduced, yet the Kilmarnock Firemen's Carnival has remained a small-town event in size. It is still owned and operated by members of the Fire Department and Ladies Auxiliary, with other local community volunteer organizations and individuals participating. Bingo has always been a centerpiece of the games. Gambling was always kept at a clean minimum—with spinning wheels of fortune for prizes or winnings of ticket chances for the big prize raffle that always ends the carnival season. Historically an automobile was the first prize for this drawing. For many years local automobile dealers offered a yearly donation, in turn, for this prize. Those cars were notably Chevrolet, Ford, or Chrysler/Plymouth products. In the forties, prior to carnival time it was customary for members of the Ladies Auxiliary to drive to towns all over the Northern Neck to sell raffle tickets for the big prize drawing at the carnival. Those early summer ticket trips were regarded by the ladies as great fun excursions. They traveled in the car that was to be the first prize in the drawing and temporary signs advertising it were placed on its top and sides. The women were highly successful in selling large amounts of tickets on these trips. My mother and her friends always participated.

Norris' Pond stands just outside of Kilmarnock, on the north end of town. It's at the foot of the hill, beside the main road (Route 3). Each winter when the pond froze, folks from all over the area came for afternoons and evenings of ice skating. Moonlight skating was especially popular. Skaters parked their cars up and down the hillside along the road near the pond. They walked around the edge of the shoreline on the south side of the pond to step onto the ice. A large barrel-fire was kept burning there for changes into skates and for warm-ups. Norris' Pond was a highlight of winter fun for everyone who could stand up on skates. Wintertime was a big disappointment when there was no ice for skating on Norris' Pond.

Dancing school brochure.

We eagerly anticipated the skating season that usually came after the Christmas holidays. It seemed that there was always something for us to do—whatever the season.

The Elcorise School of Dance was an excellent dancing school that was held uptown from 1939 to 1944. It was conducted by Elmer and Jeanne Iseman, sisters who came from Richmond to hold their dance classes on weekends during the winter months.

In the beginning, classes were held in the Dreamland dance hall on Augusta Street. But soon the school moved to the newly renovated firehouse building on East Church Street where

49

classes were held upstairs in the auditorium. A piano accompanist from their Richmond dance school came along to provide music for the lessons. There were classes in tap dance, toe dancing, and ballet, with ballroom dancing for older students. The school attracted young people from as far away as Tappahannock, Lottsburg, Reedville, and Wicomico, as well as the Kilmarnock, Irvington, White Stone, Weems, and Upper Lancaster communities. When springtime arrived, a big dance revue was held in the Kilmarnock Opera House that was upstairs in the large old Hazel Building on Main Street.

I took dance lessons for four years and remember it vividly. It was a highlight of my youth.

For classes of tap, toe, or ballet, girls wore a short royal blue cotton dress that had a flared skirt. There was a white EIC monogram embroidered on the bodice front. The little dance class dresses had wide cap sleeves at the shoulders. Tight-fitting, short, matching breeches were worn under the dresses.

Elmer Corinne Iseman was a strict and demanding dance instructor. She conducted all of her classes using a carnival cane to strike the floor for emphasis at various points in the lesson. Miss Iseman (Elmer) was ever the picture of a professional ballerina. She wore her jet-black hair parted in the center, pulled sleekly back, and caught in a flat knot low on the backside of her head. Sometimes she wore two small braided knots, one on each side of her head, near her ears. Her sister, Jeanne, served as her assistant, for Elmer was definitely the lead instructor. Clapping her hands sharply, Miss Iseman easily commanded our full attention—and I loved it.

I was both fascinated and thrilled when I first saw the large professionally drawn and colored designs for costumes that we would wear in the dance revue. The costume designs and fabrics always came from New York, and the stage sets and orchestra came from Richmond for the production. There were more than a hundred children in the classes. Costumes for all of the dancers, and for each of their routines, were sewn by one local seamstress, Mrs. Bill Green. It must've been a daunting task, but she always managed to complete all of the costumes on time. There's a printed dancing school brochure at the Kilmarnock Museum. It has a photo of Elmer Iseman, in her tu-tu, on the front cover.

I took tap, ballet, and toe lessons, but my great love for toe dancing must have earned a special spot for me with the Isemans. They had a summer cottage at Mundy Point, near Lottsburg. One summer they invited me for an overnight visit there—along with my dance classmate, Shirley Green. Her mother sewed the costumes. My recollection of that night at their cottage was of my inability to sleep because an owl was hooting in the trees outside of our bedroom window. A spooky atmosphere was created by this eerie sound. It caused a huge scare in our little ten-year-old minds. We cringed and huddled under the bedcovers as we tried to hide from the shadows of moonlight that were flickering on the walls and dancing around in the unfamiliar surroundings of our room.

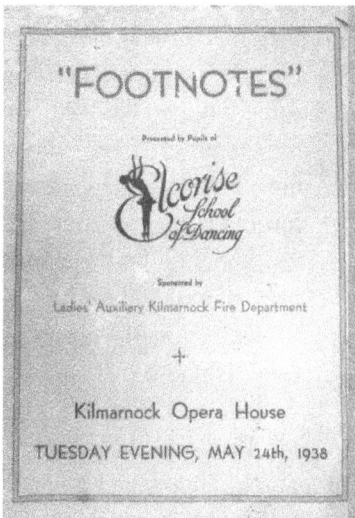

Dance revue program.

One year I had a big solo spot on the revue program. This was when I crossed the stage, on toe, going backward across the full distance of the wide stage. As I arched my back at a backward angle with my arms outstretched forward, my head dropped downward in an upside-down position. WOW! Those were the days of youthful agility. I do remember, clearly, that very special number with the trip across the stage and hearing a lot of applause as I finished. Soon after that pinnacle of my dance career, my dancing days came to a screeching halt. I remember the evening at home when I sat at the top of our living room staircase as the Isemans, with their mother accompanying them, came to call. They came to make a rare kind of proposal to my parents for taking me to New York to do something? I couldn't comprehend it all. But I knew that my dad was vehemently objecting and that the discussion soon became a very heated one. Shortly thereafter I dropped out of dancing lessons, according to the wishes of my parents, and my heart was broken. However, they made a wise decision for me, one that I could understand better as I grew older.

Years later, while on a shopping trip to Richmond in the mid 1950s,

Posing in my solo dance revue costume.

I saw Jeanne Iseman at a store where she was employed. When I asked if she was Jeanne Iseman, she replied "yes." So I told her that she and her sister, Elmer, had taught me dancing lessons. When I told her my name she immediately replied, "From Kilmarnock, Virginia." Well, I guess I made an impression, of some type, on the Isemans for them to remember me. I surely had never forgotten them. After all, toe dancing had become my "suppressed desire."

One notable business establishment uptown was the N & P Style Shop. Mr. Herbert Pilch came to Kilmarnock in the 1930s from the Philadelphia area. He opened a small dress shop at the south end of Main Street, along with Mrs. Molly Noblett. Her son was George Noblett—who won the Irish Sweepstakes when he was a young man and later became successful in the appliance business in town. Mr. Pilch and Mrs. Noblett operated the Style Shop together until her death. Afterward he continued to expand the business, making it a thriving success. In the 1940s ladies from the entire Neck, as well as a few women from Richmond, looked forward each year to his famous August sales.

One September in the 1950s the Lancaster County Junior Women's Club held an outstanding fashion show that featured his N & P Style Shop fashions. The affair was held on the waterfront lawn at Bel Air, on the Rappahannock, in Upper Lancaster County, where the Pollard family had graciously loaned their home for the site of the event.

Attractive ladies from all over the Northern Neck modeled for the show and Mr. Pilch personally selected and special-ordered each outfit from New York. He was an astute salesman with a keen sense of fashion and style. Herb Pilch was highly respected for his talents and well liked in the community.

The theme for the show was "A Trip Around the World." Pat P. Headley, who had moved to Irvington from Washington, D.C., was the mistress of ceremonies and narrator for the program, which she had scripted for the fashions. She was a multitalented lady who had been professionally associated with radio in the D.C. area. She and her (then) husband, Grayson Headley, were owners and innovators of the new WKWI radio station in Kilmarnock. The Club set up a large refreshment table on the lawn with an ocean liner centerpiece to define the theme of the show. This was a fun project for us and we used small chrysanthemum blooms to cover the hull of the boat. The show was a huge affair, attended by women from all over the Northern Neck to benefit various charities in the area.

In the early forties the Donna Lo Beauty Salon, uptown on Main Street, was the principal hair salon in the immediate area. At that time ladies were getting "permanent waves" and my mother decided that my straight hair needed curls. She took me to the Donna Lo for my first "permanent" when I was eleven or twelve years old. The long process involved first shampooing and rolling my hair on many chemically treated curling papers. Then I sat hooked up to an overhead awning affair of wiring, for what seemed like hours, while electricity heated the attached curlers. When I was finally released from the hateful contraption, the curls had been "set" and the "comb-out" could be done. All it ever did for my hair was

Suta with me and my frizzy "perm" hair, 1942.

to produce a distressing "frizzle" that caused me to cry every morning when I looked into the mirror. Finally in 1944 a new style of haircut became popular. It was called a "feather cut." It had to be done by a skilled beautician who used a razor blade for cutting the hair. Mother took me back to Donna Lo on a very hot and humid August day. The girl who gave me the new cut was named "Agnes." I'll never forget the change Agnes gave to me. A miracle had taken place. I now had "natural curls"—without any kind of chemical encouragement. The frizzy days were finally ended forever.

Rob Shearman's Hardware Store was next door to Rice's Soda Shoppe. From the 1930s, up until the town fire of 1952, it was the gathering spot for a small group of men—the "old timers" and two or three other regulars. They congregated there each and every night of the week around a big potbelly stove—to "chew the fat" and to exchange any choice bits of local gossip that they could contribute. They smoked pipes, cigars, and cigarettes, chewed a little tobacco and possibly shared a "swig" or two from a bottle of "hooch." The folksy circle of men sometimes played cards—penuckle (pinochle) was the game of choice. But the main purpose for meeting was simply conversation. It's unlikely that very much worldly wisdom was imparted, but it was the fellas' night out, which meant "every night" for some of them. They enjoyed keeping rustic country "gab fests" alive. The plate-glass front window of the store was always clouded by heavy smoke, making the murky figures inside barely visible to passersby, but roars of hearty laughter could be heard outside on the street. Some of the stories exchanged at those sessions were surely best left there around the heat of the stove.

In 1939 Leon Rice opened his Soda Shoppe on North Main Street, diagonally across from the office of the *Rappahannock Record*. It became THE popular gathering spot for many people of the area until the disastrous town fire of 1952. The shop was open six days of the week and remained open until ten o'clock each night. It was then an afternoon ritual for ladies to meet at Leon's every afternoon for a Coca-Cola. Consequently, from an early age, my mother took me with her each day to join her friends there. The businessmen of town usually ate their lunch at Leon's. I practically grew up at Leon's and learned to appreciate its uniqueness as I matured.

Leon was a neat sort of fellow, a former William and Mary College

54

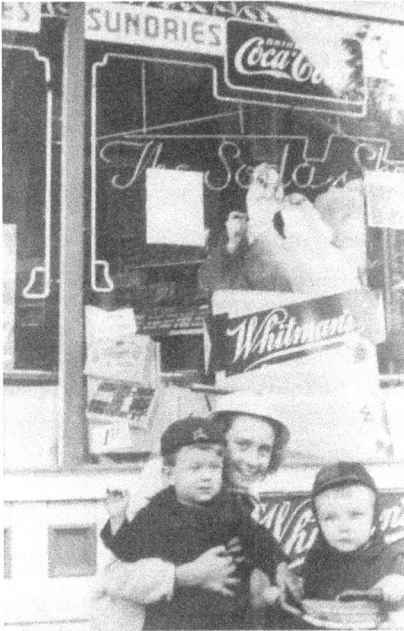

Nancy with cousin, William Beane, and Lee Rice, in front of Leon's Soda Shoppe, 1942.

student and a great lover of the Big Band music of the forties era. In his brown and white saddle shoes his toes were always tapping to the rhythms of the jukebox music. The tunes played softly in the background as they drifted through the air in his shiny and immaculate shop. I especially loved Artie Shaw and Benny Goodman music. "Amapola," and "Frenesi," and "Manhattan Serenade" were memorable songs we heard at Leon's during the wartime years. We could buy our records at his shop. He sold Columbia, Decca, Victor, and Okeh record labels with the music of Artie Shaw, Benny Goodman, Glenn Miller, Harry James, Tommy Dorsey, and the other great Big Band leaders of the era.

The atmosphere of the place made it a sort of "Mecca" where crowds gathered after seeing a movie at the Fairfax or after Elcorise dancing school lessons. Leon prepared all of the lunches himself, in his tiny closet/ kitchen. It was under the staircase that led upstairs to Bonner Hall, where the Holly Ball had been held in the 1920s. His country ham sandwiches—always with the crust trimmed off—were a specialty. He also served soups, including oyster stew, on occasion, and his mother provided homemade pies for the shop. In addition, she sewed green fabric envelope covers for the wire backs of the ice cream parlor chairs that surrounded six round tables with green painted tops. She had embroidered "The Soda Shoppe" in small red script lettering on the back of each chair cover. How could anyone forget such an amazingly simple touch of class?

Leon sold newspapers, movie and other magazines, pipes, pipe tobaccos, cigarettes, along with Ronson cigarette lighters (the popular coffee table "genie" style ones), and the (then) popular Whitman boxed candies. Other candies and a rack of postcards and sunglasses were on sale there too. His standard soda fountain treats were Coca-Cola, his wonderful limeade drinks, milk shakes, sodas, ice cream sundaes, banana splits, and "short chocolate" drinks—a favorite for the little kids.

In 1942 Leon's wife, Judy, snapped a picture of me in front of the shop—along with their son, Lee, and my cousin, William Beane. It is the only known photo of the place.

When the town fire of March 1952 destroyed most of the businesses at the north end of town, Leon's succumbed in the devastation. Its gray marble fountain did not even survive for recognition. Leon Rice never rebuilt the shop and the town lost a true icon of an era—for it was truly one of the best and quintessential soda shops of the time.

In 1995, as a former student of design and also a miniature enthusiast, I decided to create a one-inch scale model of this great shop for the Kilmarnock Museum. I began by collecting items to use and later began working on the project, which I finally completed in 2004. I wanted this beloved spot to always be remembered.

The miniature model of Leon's Soda Shoppe.

V

Church

M y parents belonged to Grace Episcopal Church in Kilmarnock. Mother joined the Episcopal Church soon after she and Daddy were married. Dad's family had always been Episcopalians. They were members of the Protestant Episcopal Church that had been formed following the disestablishment of the Anglican Church in the colonies after the Revolution. This was the reason that Christ Church, near Weems, remained abandoned for so many years.

In 1851, the new congregation of Grace Church organized and built a small frame church in Kilmarnock. The size of that church was adequate for the membership of Grace for many years. A large brick church was

Grace Church, Kilmarnock, circa 1930. *Photo courtesy of Kilmarnock Museum.*

built at the site in 1958 to accommodate a growing congregation. Grace Church members made up the congregation of old Christ Church, built in 1735. The historic old building was unheated and not used in the winter. Services were held at Christ Church in the summertime on most Sundays during the forties and on occasional summer Sundays during the thirties. The June homecoming service at Christ Church was the highlight of the Grace Church church calendar.

There were only a few young people in the small congregation at Grace Church when I was a young child, so I preferred going to Sunday school at the Baptist church in town. That was where my first-grade schoolmates, Jackie Hughes, Jeanne Blake, and Grace Ann Simmons, went to church. Mrs. Leonora Dew was the sweet lady who taught the youngest children there. Nevertheless, my parents always took me with them for services at Grace Church. Kilmarnock Methodist Church was also on Church Street and very soon I switched and began going to Sunday school there with my Irvington Road girlfriends, Rebecca Lou Dixon and the Moormans. Another incentive for me to go to the Methodist Sunday school was the dear lady who taught the youngest children there. She was Mrs. Cutler (of Irvington Road), who made birthday cakes for children in her class—and in my young mind, that made the Methodist church a very special place.

The Methodists and Baptists both conducted two weeks of Bible school every summer. I looked forward each year to this time because there were always large numbers of children who attended Bible school. Grace Church didn't hold Bible school because there were so few children there. Instead, we went to either the Baptist or Methodist Vacation Bible School.

I finally began to attend Grace Church Sunday school when I was in fifth grade. There were only three girls in my class and Mrs. Enid Turner was our teacher. Church picnics were held at the end of the summer season by each of the community churches. These picnics usually took place at the old Taft Fish Factory (no longer in operation) at Cherry Point, near White Stone. They were always very large events. The traditional picnic menu included fried chicken, hot dogs, watermelon, ice cream popsicles (Eskimo Pies), soft drinks, and iced tea.

Regarding my early Sunday school days, my dad always said that I had "tried them all, except the Catholic and Seventh-Day Adventist." They were the only other churches in town. I had been baptized at Christ Church and later was confirmed there. I clearly remember my confirmation day when Bishop Henry St. George Tucker placed his hands on my head for that service. I wore a white dress that was trimmed with Irish crocheted lace and I kept that very special dress carefully tucked away for more than sixty years afterwards. My confirmation took place on homecoming Sunday in 1942, when I was twelve years old. Naturally my gift for the occasion was my very own prayer book-hymnal that had my name embossed in gold lettering on the front cover. By that time I had become a full-fledged Episcopalian.

When we were fourteen, our little Grace Church trio, Virginia Harvey, Betty Jo Venable, and I, attended church camp in Richmond at Rosalyn Episcopal Church Conference Center. There we studied the prayer book and learned hymns that became favorites of mine. We had a lot of fun meeting other young Episcopalians from all over the state.

At Christ Church the summertime services were held at eleven o'clock on Sunday mornings. The midday heat was not a bother for us at the time, for we were not used to air conditioning in the forties. My grandmother, Nanee, always sat straight up in an erect position on her seat in the Carter family pew, or knelt to pray on a leather footstool "kneeler." As she sat in the high-backed old pew she never flinched or showed any signs of discomfort, even though the heat of the day was often oppressive.

Dressed in her hat, gloves, hosiery, and the corset that she wore under her dress, she remained placid and cool as she fanned herself with her own straw fan. Nanee was the image of Christian fortitude and towering strength as she faced life's trials and tribulations. Never ruffled by challenges and with an even-tempered nature, she was a wise decision maker. Corie, her daughter, who was always at her side, was surely her greatest cross to bear. But Nanee was steadfast in her duty to Corie.

My Sunday memories of Christ Church also include "Miss" Carrie K. Chase. We called her "Miss," though she was a widow. That's an old Southern way of addressing ladies to show affection and respect. She played the pump organ for the service in the large pew occupied by the choir. It was just across the aisle from the Carter family pew in front of the altar. The Chase family sat in the pew on the south aisle, behind the large choir pew. Two of the Chases married my grandmother's Carter siblings:

Rawleigh D. and Betty. Their Chase ancestor had arrived here in the late 1800s from the New England states.

Mrs. Enid Turner was quite visible as she stood tall above the high-back brown pew where she sat on the north aisle of the church. Each Sunday she wore a different large and colorful hat—and all of her hats had very wide brims. She was a handsome, well-dressed, and immaculately groomed lady—a conspicuous presence in the church. As a member of the Eubank family of Kilmarnock, "Miss Enid" was financially "well-heeled," the owner of much of the town's real estate. She was generous in providing funds for Grace Church's financial needs. Our church was very fortunate when Mrs. Turner donated the funds to save the small historic frame church building from demolition when the new church was built in 1958. The little church was moved several feet in order for the new one to be built on the same spot where the old one had once stood. It became Grace Chapel.

At Christ Church on homecoming Sunday the picnic food, brought by individual families, was laid out for sharing. At first it was served from the board shelf that was attached up high on the inside of the iron fence that stretched across the north side of the churchyard.

Christ Church as it was in the 1930s and 40s.

Sometime later the ladies set up buffet tables for the food close to where the Kelly tombs were located. There was a large tree there that shaded the food in the summer heat. We used the north door entrance to the church, and cars were parked on the front lawn, outside of the churchyard. People set up their bridge tables and chairs to eat lunch in the shade of the grove of trees on the front lawn.

Each year Hurst Harvey, Flex Chase, my uncle Ben, and my dad, Charlie Hubbard, were in charge of iced tea and lemonade. They served it from the back of Flex Chase's pick-up farm truck, and chipped ice from the large blocks of ice that they obtained at the nearby Irvington ice plant.

Homecoming was when a large number of the members of Trinity Church, in Lancaster, and St. Mary's White Chapel joined with Grace Church members for a parish reunion. Many relatives returned from afar for the occasion as well. It was an important event in our parish life every year.

In the 1930s, services at Grace Church during the winter months were warm and cozy. The small space inside of the little building was heated by a wood-burning stove. Services were conducted in a reverent, but low-church simple form using the 1928 Prayer Book Service. Miss Carrie was at the pump organ providing music for a choir made up of six or seven people, mostly ladies. I was one of two or three children who sang in the choir for a short time. The Christmas candlelight service was my favorite. The small congregation at Grace was a close-knit church family, sharing both happy and sad events with joy or compassion.

Mother served on the altar guild and Daddy served on the vestry. In the early years, Nanee had been the first president of the Ladies' Aid Society. For a few years in the 1950s the ladies of the Women's Auxiliary served dinner in the new parish house to the men of the local Rotary Club. This was a big undertaking for the small band of women. They planned, shopped, and then prepared the meals in the parish house kitchen, cooking on the large commercial-sized gas stove there. Dishwashing was done in the small sink, with all of the china and utensils hand-dried by the women. There was virtually no counter space in that first kitchen. The ladies served a full dinner to about sixty men each and every Friday night—with no more than a total of twelve workers. The Rotary dinners were a major fundraising project for the ECW (Episcopal Church Women). My mother was in charge of all grocery purchasing, as well as participating in the food preparations and serving. It was a very successful financial endeavor for these valiant ladies. However, I do believe that they became weary and were relieved when the Rotarians sought to move to a larger location. It had been an exhausting enterprise, but they had cheerfully and faithfully accomplished the mission.

Bazaar, rummage, and bake sales were other moneymaking events held in the parish house in those years, as well as a few other activities. But no bridge parties were allowed in the parish house for many years. The only alcoholic beverage served at church functions during those years was the wine of the holy communion service. The new parish house (built in 1948) had been the gift of one lady, Mrs. Fanny Beeler Chase Staton, who lived in North Carolina and was a distant relative of some of the Grace Church members. She had stipulated in making her gift that there should be no card games or alcohol served in the building. In later years, this rather limiting decree was lifted after the parish house was enlarged and renovated through funding provided by the congregation.

Our Grace Church family during the Great Depression and throughout the World War II years was a small yet mighty and active community force. The simplicity of the service itself, as well as the dignity and gentleness that characterized our small town church family life, were deeply meaningful for me.

VI

Stepping Out 'n' Tripping Around

In the thirties, when I was very young, an exciting summer event was the arrival of Adams Floating Theatre. It was a special treat to step on board and see live actors on stage in a theatre that was on a BOAT! It always docked at the Irvington wharf—next to the ferryboat, which, at that time, operated from the landing at the foot of the hill, below Irvington Beach Hotel.

Getting a box of Cracker Jacks at the floating theatre was very important to my little girlfriends and me. We seemed compelled to compare the prizes that we got in our boxes. I don't remember what the tiny prizes were, but they served to promote a lot of review and discussion among us over who had gotten the best prize in our box. Cracker Jacks were new treats for us—and they first came to us on the floating theatre.

In the thirties, late forties and early fifties, another big summer event was the Irvington Fourth of July celebration. People came from all over the Northern Neck for the full day of festivities. There were baseball games galore with teams representing towns from the lower end of the Neck. The powerboat races were the biggest attraction.

Boats of several classes participated: workboats, yachts, and speedboats. There were no sailboats in these races, which took place on Carter's Creek, and the races were very noisy and competitive. They were exciting events. Large crowds stood on private piers along the creek and on the dock at the Rappahannock River Yacht Club to get a full view of the action. Loud cheers could be heard with enthusiastic talk among the onlookers as they discussed the outcome of each race.

My family and friends always stood on the Yacht Club dock to view the spectacle. We watched as the speedboats raced by—bobbing and spouting their fountain sprays of water with noise that was deafening to our ears. The drone and din of the loud motors was coupled with the noxious odor of gasoline fumes and heavy drifts of smoky air. As the little boats raced round and round, their motors seemed to imitate the annoying buzz of large ornery mosquitoes zooming around our ears. We anxiously watched the drivers as they fiercely held onto the steering wheels of their tiny boats. We feared that one of the drivers might pop up and be flung overboard by the force of hitting another boat's wake in the water. The racers were flipping high in their seats and appeared to be much like horseback riders jumping high fence rails. We thought that the speedboat races were the best. They created more excitement for everyone. The workboat or yacht races had more appeal for people who knew participants in those classes.

The sprawling little town had only a few streets that spread out in lengthy directions of east and west. Crowds milled about throughout each end of town during the day, attending different events. Hot dogs and soft drinks were sold at intermittent spots along the way. It was a day to see everyone you knew and definitely plenty of people that you didn't know.

In the late afternoon a beauty pageant was held and "Miss Rappahannock" was chosen by a judging committee. The candidates were young girls who represented their towns on the river.

In 1948 Richmond Mayor Horace Edwards crowned my friend, Sylvia Mae Kilduff, the new Miss Rappahannock. She was also crowned Holly Ball Queen the same year at that Christmas event held in Kilmarnock.

Miss Rappahannock and her court of attendants rode on a large buy-boat that was decorated for the occasion. It motored from a branch of Carter's Creek to the same pier where the floating theatre had docked— near the old ferry dock at the east end of town. The coronation was held there. Little girls serving as flower girls were also aboard with the queen's court. They were chosen by the celebration committee. Once I was one of the flower girls and remember how beautiful I thought Miss Rappahannock looked. I'm sure that she was Madeline Fisher, from Ocran, who was known locally for her beauty. The queen and her court attendants wore full-length, pastel-colored organdy dresses and carried large arm bouquets of garden flowers. The flower girls all wore dresses similar to the attendants and carried small baskets of flowers. Senator R. O. Norris usually did the honors of crowning all queens at area events. He was a colorful and eloquent speaker, so he probably made the coronation address that year when I was a flower girl. I was about five years old, so remember very little about speech making. But I do remember the things that impressed me: clothes, colors, flowers, and beauty—as well as the boat ride filled with pageantry.

The coronation of Miss Rappahannock took place at the end of the day, following the conclusion of all of the boat races and ball games. Nightfall brought forth an exciting display of fireworks. Many folks lingered for this final spectacle at the end of the long day of celebration.

As the Irvington Fourth of July celebration continued into the fifties, changes took place in the Miss Rappahannock pageant. The beauty pageant became a bathing beauty contest. Contestants no longer wore the full-length dresses. In 1950 the event was staged aboard the *High Tide*, the luxury yacht of The Tides Inn. That year my childhood playmate, Frances Moorman, was crowned Miss Rappahannock. The passage of time brought even more changes in the program and style of Irvington's Fourth celebration.

Each September in the thirties and forties, all of us kids eagerly awaited our family trip to the Virginia State Fair that was held in Richmond. The variety of rides at the fair was more exciting than the carnival rides at home. I liked the funhouse and seeing motorcycle riders whirling round and round inside a deep, wooden, bowl-like structure. I was amazed by their wild riding, but was frightened by the noise and vibrations that they created inside of the bowl. As we walked along the midway I had an eye-opening experience when I saw the fat lady and gypsy fortunetellers. It was a glimpse into a world that was totally foreign to me. I was curious about these people, but my parents always said "no" to attending any of the sideshows. Cotton candy was sweet and messy to eat—a completely different kind of treat. They didn't have it at our Firemen's Carnival at home. The hot dogs and popcorn tasted especially good to me at the fair, too. When we came home all of us kids had great fun telling each other about what we had seen and done at the state fair. That was an all-important part of the trip. We were very careful to blow our stories into tales of high drama as we related them to our audience.

When I was about eight years old, my parents took me for a weekend trip to Virginia Beach. I was very excited that I was going to go swimming in the ocean for the first time. It would be different from our river swimming and I looked forward to having fun jumping in the big waves. We stayed at the Greenwood cottage on the oceanfront. My enthusiasm was dashed, however, when a "nor'easter" storm rendered our entire weekend a complete washout. I was crushed that the rains prevented my much-anticipated frolic in ocean waves. This was definitely a big disappointment. But it was an early lesson in navigating one of life's unpredictable misfortunes, one that even an only child must learn.

One summer I had an unforgettable adventure when I took an exciting trip to the mountains of Virginia with my girlfriend, Virginia Dix McGinnes. She lived at Bertrand, at the upper end of Lancaster County. Her mother, Aileen, often came and fetched me to spend time at their home to play with Virginia. She was near my age and had no girl playmates in the vicinity of their home. Her brother, Frank, was seven years older, so Aileen realized that Virginia needed to have some girlfriends. I always had fun visiting Virginia. Her home was on the Corotoman River and distant from my normal activities at home. A visit with Virginia always provided different kinds of experiences in the remote setting of the upper part of the county. On one of my summer visits with Virginia, Aileen taught me to swim at the sandy beach across the inlet in front of their house. Once she arranged for us to get up early in the morning to see the sun rising over the river. On another visit she made sure that we were awake at night when we could view the northern lights, or the aurora borealis. I was fascinated with that new term, "aurora borealis," so I repeated it over and over, though I'm sure that my pronunciation was unrecognizable. I still think the term has a rhythmic cadence to it.

Aileen McGinnes was a well-known personality throughout Lancaster County and the Northern Neck. She had a reputation for being interesting and unpredictable with a dynamic way of approaching life. Her varied interests often motivated her to quick action whenever she discovered a new idea that she thought would be worthwhile to pursue.

On this infamous mountain trip, Virginia Dix and I were about nine years old. Mrs. McGinnes decided that we should go with her to show the mountains of Virginia to her lady friend who was visiting from out of the state. We traveled in a Chevy car that had no air conditioning, of course, and all of the windows in the car were left wide open for the trip. When Virginia and I jumped in to sit on the backseat of the car, we were promptly joined by a box of three healthy, very live and very active, white leghorn chickens whose legs were all tied together. Her mother placed the open cardboard box with the hens on the backseat between us. These feathered riding companions provided us with a lively and entertaining ride, all the way to Charlottesville. They became agitated by the windy conditions in the car and their wings flapped furiously as they spent the entire drive excitedly trying to rise up and out of the box. That rising and falling, with their wings flapping wildly, made the long ride a pins-and-needles affair for me. When we reached Charlottesville, Mrs. McGinnes parked the car, took the box with the chickens, walked down the street and shortly returned to the car without the hens. I never knew what she had done with the chickens or why they had been a part of the journey. But my heart was leaping with joy by their absence as we continued on our drive toward the mountains.

Motels were nowhere to be seen in those days but "Mrs. Mac" spied the Sunset Motel nestled in a distant nook of the mountainside. The cinder block building was painted bright orange with the picture of a sunset emblazoned on the front of the building. The Sunset became our nighttime refuge and another broadening experience had begun for me. Since no reservations had been made, we were lucky to find that resting spot. I was homesick before we returned because I had left home to spend two nights with Virginia and by that time I had been away for nearly a week. Mother had sent me off with my toothbrush, sandals and two sunsuits. That was definitely my most exciting visit to Virginia's house.

For several summers in the 1940s, my parents sent me to spend two or three weeks at Seashore Camp for Girls at Virginia Beach. It was a small private girls' camp located at the far end of the beach, close to Fort Story military base. Our camp was situated on the oceanfront in a large one-story shingled cottage that had a screened sleeping porch that wrapped around the building. Genevieve Gresham White, the owner of the camp, had previously lived in our area. I loved Seashore Camp.

It was wartime (World War II) and there were some notable sights and occurrences pertaining to the war that colored my camp days.

The first of these was my ride from home to camp with "T" Waller. One year, due to wartime gas rationing, my parents arranged for me to ride to camp with their friend, "T" Waller, who was returning to his naval duty in Hampton Roads after spending a weekend leave at his home in Reedville.

He was a tall, dark, and handsome ensign. I was a shy, impressionable little "teeny-bopper" of eleven or twelve years old. On the ride he offered to share part of his roast beef sandwich that his mother had prepared for him at home. I was overcome with embarrassment by his offer and moved as far away from him as possible on the front seat of the car. It was a wonder that I didn't cause the door to pop open. I could sense that my face had turned bright red and I tried desperately to keep my head turned in the opposite direction, hoping that he wouldn't spy my flushed cheeks. For many years afterward, whenever "T" and I met we had a good laugh about that car ride. At the time of the ride he had been dating my favorite counselor at camp, which was the reason why he could deliver me to Camp Seashore. Her name was Nancy Pierpont and I thought that she was gorgeous. To me, she looked like Ingrid Bergman, the movie star.

At nighttime, blackout was strictly enforced so there were never any lights burning in the cottage or on the sleeping porch. This didn't present any hardships though; we were in our bunks by eight o'clock and asleep before dark. A counselor came around with a flashlight during the night to check on our well-being. Early in the morning we woke up and ran to the beach for a shocking wake-up dip in the cold ocean water, followed by flag-raising on the beach with the Pledge of Allegiance.

A new camp friend of mine was from Washington, D.C. Her name was Katherine Holmes and her uncle was presidential secretary, Steven Early, under President Roosevelt. I liked her a lot and was very flattered to be a friend of anyone with such important worldly connections. The only person that was familiar to me who had been in high government affairs was our Northern Neck native son, George Washington.

One day in 1942—as we were making mud castles and playing on the beach—we saw floating debris coming ashore from a sunken ship. No doubt it had come from a sunken merchant ship, which was something that was quietly taking place not far from the Virginia coast during that period in the war. Some of it appeared to be human body parts. To us, this was a horribly shocking and unforgettable sight. It occurred to us, at the time, that what we were seeing wash up on our beach could have come from such an event, yet the war seemed far away from us—happening on the other side of the ocean—where we saw the big warships heading each day. We couldn't believe that the war was anywhere near us.

Seashore Camp was only three or flour blocks from Fort Story and often, in the late afternoon, Italian prisoners of war were brought to play volleyball in front of our camp, where there was a net set up on the beach. We were never in danger or afraid of those prisoners. They were closely guarded by the military police (MP's). We were intrigued, both by their Italian language and by the vigorous way that they played the game. It was quite a sight to see them bouncing the ball off of their shoulders, chests, knees, and sometimes even off of their heads. They seemed to be extremely happy, loudly shouting and laughing as they played. It appeared to us that they regarded their incarceration as a holiday from war—they were obviously enjoying themselves. But we never learned why Italian prisoners were at Fort Story.

We were allowed to take the city bus one afternoon of the week to go uptown to get postcards and see a movie. One of those was *The Dolley Sisters*. The stars were Betty Grable and Gloria de Haven and I thought they looked almost like twins. I loved the movie—the music and dancing were the attraction for me.

On one of those afternoon trips uptown, several of us decided that we would stand outside of the Princess Anne Hotel to get a glimpse of Harry James (the bandleader) and Betty Grable (the movie star). We had heard that they were honeymooning there and we were absolutely sure that we would see them. After waiting for most of our afternoon uptown, we missed our sighting. Naturally, we were crushed beyond words. We finally had to catch a city bus and ride back to camp wondering, "Could we have gotten a wrong report about their Virginia Beach honeymoon?"

Mrs. White offered a campers' trip to New York at the end of each camp season. In 1942 I went on this trip along with a hometown friend, Betty Jo Venable.

The group met at Norfolk, where we boarded an Old Bay Line steamboat for the overnight trip up the Bay to Baltimore. From there we rode the train to New York. This was all in the way of introducing us to travel experience, and what a wonderful experience it was!

On the rumbling overnight steamboat ride my little travel companion decided that she didn't like going so far away from home. She cried all night in her stateroom bunk above mine, generally making my steamboat trip a lot less thrilling. I wasn't the least bit homesick. It was a great adventure for me to be going to New York. Riding on a steamboat was entirely different from our boat rides on the river and the train ride was to be my very first one.

There were about fifteen girls taking the trip, chaperoned by three of the camp counselors. In New York we stayed at the Taft Hotel and ate a few times at The Automat. This was a new idea to us. We had never seen food that was displayed inside of a glass post-office type box. We eagerly made our selections and waited for the window to open so that we could retrieve our food. The Automat was a fun place to eat.

We saw the sights: the Statue of Liberty; the Empire State Building; Chinatown; a stage play, *Life With Father*; Radio City Music Hall and the Rockettes; the *Hellzapoppin* stage show; and a radio broadcast, which was the highlight for me.

The show's master of ceremonies was Harry von Zell, who introduced a new singer to the audience. The singer had shoulder length hair with a big pouf of bangs on her forehead. As she came to the microphone he introduced, "Miss Dinah Shore." She was wearing a blue lace evening dress that was exactly like my mother's dress back at home. I could never forget the thrill of that moment—to see a "big New York singer" wearing a dress like my mother's! I only wish that we had saved the dress for posterity. I think she sang, "Don't Sit Under the Apple Tree," but the dress that she was wearing took precedence, in my mind, over the song that she sang. I was twelve years old at the time.

Richmond was the destination for everyone in our lower part of the Northern Neck to do any major shopping or for hospital care. I went to Richmond for my tonsillectomy in the thirties and traveled the same route for the hospital delivery of my first two children in the early fifties. This was common practice in our area. Infants were also delivered in the doctors' offices here.

Without a bridge at the lower end of the Northern Neck, our route to Richmond was through Tappahannock, where we crossed the Rappahannock over the Downing Bridge. When I was very young I usually became carsick on every shopping trip to Richmond. I always dreaded the long two-hour drive, although I eagerly looked forward to going to the city. We traveled armed with a fresh lemon for me to nurse as a remedy for my carsickness. This never kept me from experiencing the effects of motion sickness. At the time there were no known medicinal remedies for the ailment. I'm sure those rides were trials for my parents, attending to me with many "sick" stops along the way. Fortunately, when we arrived in the city, my illness faded and I could tag along for the day of shopping without causing more distress. It was a strange development that the return trip was pleasantly uneventful. I was a tired and sleepy little girl—too tired to get sick, I guess.

Since I was an only child, my parents carried me with them on nearly every outing that they took. They carried me along when they went to see the first Richmond showing of *Gone with the Wind* at Loew's Theatre in 1939. I did a lot of sleeping during the long hours of the movie, but do remember how I loved the old-fashioned clothes worn in the film. Afterward Mother and Daddy gave me a book of the *Gone with the Wind* paper dolls to cut out and dress.

A day trip for shopping in Richmond was a regular outing for many of us. Ladies would get together and take their children with them on seasonal shopping trips. We also went shopping "in town" as a family. My dad liked to shop at Greentrees. He loved clothes and often went there to get outfitted in the late forties. My dad was a dapper dresser—meant to be a city fellow. Mother took me along for shopping at Miller & Rhoads and Thalhimers. These were the two big department stores that attracted shoppers from all over the state. I liked watching mother shop for cosmetics at the Charles of the Ritz counter in Miller & Rhoads. There the legendary Mrs. Orr mixed special formula face powder for my mother and other women. I was fascinated by the way that she mixed different shades of powders. It looked like she was mixing ingredients for cooking. I think that mother must have been one of Mrs. Orr's best customers because she faithfully used the program of "C of R" cosmetics up until her death in the eighties.

When it was a "lady day" trip, the women always planned to meet for lunch in the Tea Room at the Miller & Rhoads department store. Eddie Weaver's organ music and the runway fashion show were the big attractions there. The food was good and there were several especially popular items on the menu. I always ordered the delicious chicken pot pie. Chocolate silk pie topped the dessert favorites. We always saw many other people that we knew eating in the Tea Room.

In the 1930s and 40s, ladies dressed up in hat and gloves for the downtown shopping excursion and their little daughters did the same. It was considered "taboo" to be seen dressed otherwise.

With the coming of the Christmas season, it was customary for many children who lived within driving distance of Richmond to visit Santa Claus at Miller & Rhoads. He was widely believed to be the "real Santa," and most parents made the trip to dutifully acknowledge that fact to their children. For me, it was always a long and tiring day of shopping with mother and then standing in long lines before I could see Santa to give him my "want list" of toys, but I loved it anyway.

As I grew older, sometimes we took one of my girlfriends with us to Richmond on a shopping trip. On one of these trips, when I was about fifteen, I took my best friend, Jeanne Blake, and we had a great day in the city. We shopped at Thalhimers and Miller & Rhoads and then walked down Sixth Street to the Virginia Record Shop to buy records—the Big Band tunes, of course. There we could go into a glass-walled listening room where we could hear the records before we made our purchases. The listening room was great fun and different from buying records at home in Kilmarnock.

Jeanne Blake (right) and me, shopping on Broad Street in Richmond, Virginia, 1946.

The day that Jeanne went with me we were photographed on Broad Street by a street photographer. He snapped our photo as we walked by the stores laden with our packages of shopping loot. These photographers were a common presence on city streets in the thirties and forties.

That day we also went to see a movie at Loew's Theatre. We loved joining in the sing-alongs to Eddie Weaver's organ music there. This took place before the feature film was shown. When the big Wurlitzer organ rose up from the orchestra pit, Eddie was playing it and the words for the songs simultaneously appeared on the movie screen. The audience joined in and sang the songs as he played. When he finished the program he turned to face the audience, flinging his legs up and over the organ bench, waving a salute to bid us farewell. He turned and the organ sank again into the orchestra pit with Eddie playing a fading chord of notes: the houselights dimmed and the movie appeared on the screen. Eddie Weaver's organ music at Loew's was always an extra treat as a part of our shopping day. When we left the theater we bought kettle corn to take home. A fellow sold it on the street, just outside of the theater.

After every shopping trip to Richmond it was customary, almost an unwritten rule, that we must take home a seven-layer chocolate cake from Thalhimers in its trademark black and white checkerboard box. Before we left town we met the rest of our traveling group "under the clock" inside of Miller & Rhoads or on the balcony in the store. On the long drive home we loved showing off our purchases to everyone who was riding in the car. This capped the day and made it all a worthwhile excursion.

The lure of the shoppers' heaven of downtown Richmond department stores and Loew's Theatre made going there a travel tradition for all Virginians—and we "Northern Neckers" were no exception.

VII

Christmas Magic

In the thirties and forties, as Christmastime approached, my mother's kitchen, like most others, was filled for weeks ahead with preparations for the season. She began getting ready before Thanksgiving. First she cut up candied fruits and nuts for her Christmas fruitcake—the dark one was her specialty. She baked it about a month before the start of the holidays. Then she drenched it with a generous dose of whiskey, nestled a few apple quarters snugly around it, carefully wrapped it in a soft cloth, and allowed it to rest. She had a special heavy container that was perfect for storing and priming the cake for its delectable holiday debut. She made cookies closer to Christmas and kept them tightly sealed in metal cookie tins.

It was important to get the right country ham for Christmas. Not all "cures" were the same. Our friends, Hugh and Garland Norris, at Norris Bros. Grocery, always reserved a delicious "old ham" for us. They knew who the people were who cured the best country ham—at least, it seemed that way to us. This custom was just one of the wonderful courtesies that we enjoyed by living in the country. Later, in the fifties, John Robert Cockrell's Super Market "looked after us" in the same way.

At our house, we started the day of feasting on Christmas morning with a breakfast of steamed salt mackerel fish served with cornmeal griddlecakes and plenty of country butter. It was also important to get homemade butter from the "right" person, a person who made butter that wasn't too salty.

Many times Mother or Nanee made plum pudding for the Christmas dinner dessert. It was always served with hard sauce that was spiked with whiskey. Mother also made a fresh coconut cake. She shredded the coconut herself. Nanee always baked a mincemeat pie for dessert and sometimes served her homemade wine jelly, but I was too young to like that. The family Christmas dinner menu always included oyster cocktail, turkey with dressing, sliced old ham, cranberry sauce, homemade pickles (cucumber, peach, and watermelon), mashed potatoes, sweet potato casserole (topped with marshmallows), green beans or peas, a congealed salad, and Parkerhouse rolls.

Christmas week was a round of Christmas dining. We went from one relative's home to another and each served a similar menu. We ate two feasts on Christmas Day: we had one at either our house or at Waterview; and we always had Christmas night dinner at Aunt Celeste's home in Lancaster. During the rest of the week we went for other dinners with each of the other nearby relatives. I especially loved the cold thick custard drink at Aunt Celeste's house. I thought it was a special treat. She served it in "Mee-Ma's" (my grandmother Beane's) footed glass punch bowl and made it from Mee-Ma's recipe. The bowl of custard was a pretty sight too, there on the serving table in her dining room, surrounded by slices of dark fruitcake. She added a little sprig of holly on the tray for decoration. It was truly a very festive sight to behold.

In the thirties and forties all of this eating in one week was the seasonal highlight for our large family. It's no wonder that so many of the men in the family succumbed to heart ailments in their youth. Little was known of the dangers of cholesterol at that time. Those eating habits were dangerous and unhealthy customs of the time.

On Christmas Eve I loved to go to the midnight service at Grace Church. The tiny church was always packed with people. Candles glowed where they sat on the narrow ledges of each window, surrounded by fresh sprigs of holly. It is surely one of God's miracles that a fire never occurred in the church on that holy night. We sang Christmas carols and then everyone took communion. The aromas that permeated the air as all of us sat snugly pressed together on the pews made it perfectly obvious that holiday spirits had been enjoyed by several people in the congregation before they arrived at church. Nevertheless, the congregation participated reverently throughout the solemn service and we all came away feeling uplifted by the joy of the holy season.

At our house, the Christmas tree stood in the alcove underneath the staircase in our living room. We didn't decorate the tree until Christmas Eve. This was the customary tree decorating time for most people, as we would be celebrating Christmas all of the coming week. Metallic icicles dripped from every branch and gave a silvery glow to the lights of the colored bulbs. My favorites were the shaped bulbs. Some were shaped like Japanese lanterns and others were like Santas. One was a dirigible and another was even a "Betty Boop." I do wish that we had saved those treasures.

Our tree was not the only scene of colored lights. It was the customary way for people everywhere in the country to decorate for Christmas. Strings of colored lights hung at intervals across the main streets of nearly every little town in the Northern Neck. Christmas was a magical time here in "God's Country."

As time moved on, the colored lights were replaced by white ones that seemed to create a more elegant and serene brilliance for the sacred season. We had moved out of the period of Art Deco decoration and were becoming more sophisticated in our taste.

VIII

Wartime

When World War II began, life changed on Irvington Road, as it did everywhere else in the country.

The shocking news that came on December 7, 1941, made an indelible mark in the minds of people living all across the United States.

For me, the news came when our family was returning from our usual Sunday dinner at Waterview Farm. Daddy stopped the car at Burke's Esso Station in White Stone, to "get a pack of Lucky's." When he came back to the car he said, "We're in it—the Japs have bombed Pearl Harbor." Mother broke into tears. I was eleven years old and immediately my fearful thought was, "My daddy will have to go to war." The news had come over the radio in the service station.

The most significant change that affected nearly every family was the draft—the conscription of young men for service in the army.

Daddy's brother, Ben, was drafted into the Army. He had been postmaster at the White Stone post office, so he became attached to the Army postal department and served his military duty in France. My dad's age—he was several years older than Ben—kept him from military service by missing the draft age for conscription. His home front service was the necessary tending of the farm by raising much-needed grain and farm products for the war effort. This was the case for all of those who were farming throughout the nation.

Wartime brought about new activities: at home, in school, and in the community—for children as well as for adults. It fostered huge changes in the daily lives of everyone.

Rationing was a new condition of life and it affected us all. We had rationing books and stamps for nearly everything: meat, foods, coffee, sugar, gas, shoes, nylon hosiery, and automobile tires. Ladies wore heavy cotton stockings instead of nylon hose. The nylon fibers were used in making parachutes for the military. Recipes were developed using honey and corn syrup as sugar substitutes in cooking. Rubber tires were simply unavailable - except for emergency needs. Sometimes black-market dealing was suspected. At those times whispers circulated around the small community regarding a few people who were able to obtain certain unavailable products or a larger quantity of rationed items than allowed. Those people were cast in an ugly and unpatriotic light that made them highly unpopular personalities.

Many people had "victory gardens" because there was a wartime shortage of food supplies. Ours was on the empty corner lot next to our house. My dad worked the garden with a manual push plow. The garden was large, so it was surely hard and exhausting work. Mother canned the garden vegetables using her large pressure cooker canner, which produced a steamy, hot kitchen. There was only a small electric circulating fan to cool the air. Canning food was a standard operation that most women all over the nation participated in throughout the war years. Shortages of food, and just about everything, were the wartime norm, but everyone pulled together and few ever complained. This generation had experienced the Great Depression and understood "doing without." There was no shortage of patriotism. People were willing to do whatever was necessary to win the war.

Pressure canner and jars, like Mother used.

At school we collected tinfoil. We rolled tinfoil scraps into balls and added to the ball, trying to see who could create the largest ball of tinfoil for the "war effort." It became a contest for us. All cigarette packages were sources of tinfoil on the inside wrapper—as were tinfoil chewing gum wrappers, which we also collected.

American women became engaged in knitting for the "Bundles for Britain" program. Women and young girls all across our country were busy knitting wool caps, afghans, scarves, and sweaters to provide the warmth of wool items that would be useful to the Brits who were suffering massive air raid attacks by the Germans. I learned to knit afghan squares when I was in fifth grade. We girls had our own small group competition to see who could knit the greatest number of those squares, but we never competed for a prize.

People bought war stamps and bonds. They were sold at banks, post offices, and other places as big promotions for funding the military needs of our country. It was very popular to buy and fill as many war stamp books (for war bonds) as one could afford. They were popular prizes, as well as gift items for all occasions.

At nighttime we drew our window curtains tightly, creating blackout curtains. Regular air raid tests were conducted by the sounding of the town fire alarm system. Civilian defense included the Ground Observer Corps, or airplane spotter defense.

Ground Observer armband worn by volunteers.

My mother and another lady were volunteer observers. The site of their lookout post was at Bluff Point, on the Bay, outside of Kilmarnock. The plane spotting station was a tiny building that sat high above ground. It was equipped with a telephone, plane identification posters, handbooks, and binoculars. Two people manned the post for each shift. They reported any planes they saw by hand cranking the telephone to call a command post in Norfolk, giving the direction of the aircraft's course, identification of the aircraft, its location, and the time of the call report. The station was manned twenty-four hours each day, by men as well as women. They were given armbands and pins that identified them as members in the Ground Observer Corps. Looking back, I doubt that many of the volunteers could accurately identify many planes, but at least they reported the warning information to the central command post. One of my friends and I often went with our mothers when they were serving their morning spotter duty. We spent the time playing in the sand near the station house.

Many ladies enrolled in Red Cross first aid classes and my mother was one of them. My dad served in the Volunteer Coast Guard Auxiliary. We had a motorboat, and many men who owned motorboats served in that capacity to help defend our shores, should the need arise.

The radio was our main media source for getting the latest war news and also for entertainment. Here in our area, WTAR radio station in Norfolk was the station with the best reception on the airwaves. We listened to it constantly. Each weekday night—at nine o'clock—my parents faithfully tuned in to hear Gabriel Heatter's radio newscast. I vaguely remember when my parents were talking about a shocking flash of war news. I recall them saying something about "Germans going in" and "breaking of glass." I was sitting at the top of our staircase, with my young ears perked to hear. At the time it came as an appalling piece of news and was not anything that I could understand as a child—not to mention the disbelief and horror held by the rest of the world. The radio newscasts kept me anxiously listening whenever the draft age was elevated. I feared that my daddy would be called to go. As it turned out, he was always a bit older than the latest age limit set for draftees into the Army.

On Saturday nights I listened to the "Hit Parade" on the radio. That was the Lucky Strike tobacco show that gave the ratings of the ten most popular songs of each week. I was always ready, with pad and pencil, to record the position number of each of the top ten tunes as they were played on the hit song list. It was fun to keep track and record the numbers from week to week—something like a game to play. Phyllis Keane was a friend of mine who often shared Saturday night "Hit Parade" with me.

I also listened to a late night radio station for music that came from Charlotte, North Carolina. The program was called "Night Mayor's Office." It played all of the Big Band music. In my early teens I lay in the darkness of my bedroom to hear that music playing softly on my tiny white bakelite Arvin radio, which sat on the table at my bedside.

Our front porch was the place where I loved to be in the summertime. It was a cozy place where the tall shrubs outside provided a cocoon of privacy. As a teeny-bopper, I sat there on the porch glider sewing clothes for my little mannequin doll (the same size as today's Barbie doll). I spent many happy hours creating for my doll while I listened to the rhythmic melodies of Big Band music. Later my piano lessons enabled me to play some of those sheet-music tunes with my rather inept keyboard ability. The beat of that music still fills my soul with nostalgia for those wonderful band sounds.

I also passed many a summer day during the war years lying on that porch glider and reading books. They were the days when I was reading *Huckleberry Finn, The Last Days of Pompeii, Heidi, Little Women,* and plenty of Nancy Drew and other mystery series books of the time.

As the war progressed I began collecting newspaper headlines and front-page covers of *Time* magazine (with its colored images of wartime figures) for a scrapbook of the war. Unfortunately, only small parts of the scrapbook survived amidst my hoard of memorabilia.

Many, many times we kids ran outdoors to look up in the sky when hundreds of Flying Fortresses flew over our little town. Kilmarnock was near Norfolk and Langley Air Base on the coast and not far from Washington, D.C., the nation's capitol. We could easily recognize those B-17 four-engine airplanes, with two motors on each wing. We always wondered where they were heading when there was such a large number of them flying together in formation.

On one of those days when the planes were flying high overhead, my friend Jeanne's young cousin, Bertram Chase (the school principal's son), pointed up to the planes and proclaimed, "I'm going to fly planes someday!" And he surely did just that. He grew up, joined the Navy, became a flyer and finally attained the rank of rear admiral. Long after World War II, in the eighties, Bert was Commander of Amphibious Forces, 7th Fleet, and Commander of Special Forces, 7th Fleet. In 1990, because of his outstanding service to Thailand, Bert was knighted by the King of Thailand and given title of "Knight Commander" in the Royal Order of the White Elephant, which was the term denoting a rank of highest order. He'd been inspired to fly during World War II.

Because automobiles were unavailable for purchase during the war years, my dad rejuvenated the old Hudson Terraplane car that had been stored in the Waterview garage. I learned to drive that car when I was fourteen, the year when I got my driver's license. The old car was like a

Sitting with Mother on the old Terraplane, our wartime car, 1944.

tin can—a very boxy and wide tin can. It had a red warning light on the dashboard that flashed intermittently and said, "NOT," for "not charging." The car bucked forward and stopped—repeatedly—until the motor was revved enough to move ahead. Unquestionably, I had an adventure in learning to drive a car. There were so few cars on the road that chugging along in the Terraplane at a mighty top speed of thirty mph seemed almost euphoric.

During these years there were war movies and musicals being shown at the Fairfax, just as at theaters everywhere else in the United States. Special prayer services were held at all churches. Early in the war our Grace Church rector, Rev. Lee Milton, became known as the "Flying Parson" for his part in ferrying planes to Great Britain on the Lend-Lease program.

There were diversions from wartime that colored our youth during these years. On Sunday afternoons, in the fall or spring, we teenagers entertained ourselves roller-skating around town. We also did a lot of bike riding. A Sunday afternoon Tea Dance affair was held for teenagers.

I believe the Cotillion-like event was sponsored by Grace Church. It was surely an effort to teach us to conduct ourselves properly at social functions. The boys dressed in coat and tie, while girls dressed in a "dressy dress," wearing hose and high-heel shoes. The "baby doll" was a popular shoe style of the day and learning to navigate in the high spike heels was painful. Jukebox music played and chaperones observed while we learned how to "break" and exchange partners politely. Most of us were completely bored with the tea dancing. We weren't jitterbugging and that, after all, was what was fun to us. Tea Dances were short lived. They lasted only one or two winters.

In the summertime we often rode our bikes to White Stone Beach and spent the day. We carried picnic lunches, sunned ourselves for hours on the dock, and spent the afternoons dancing on the pavilion dance floor to jukebox music. Most memorable of those tunes were "Route 66," "South America, Take It Away," "Drinkin' Rum and Coca-Cola" (by the Andrews Sisters, of course), "Beer Barrel Polka," and "One O'Clock Jump."

Before the days when we danced at the Beach, our mothers had car-pooled, due to wartime gas rationing, to take us to the Beach for our swimming. They had gathered on the pavilion porch where they sat lined up in a row of Adirondack chairs to watch us while they drank their Coca-Colas and smoked cigarettes. No sophisticated country club setting, to be sure, but White Stone Beach provided a rustic sort of resort life, which was our Northern Neck style of country living.

On infrequent occasions sailors from the Navy boats that were practicing in the Bay came to the Beach on shore leave. My age group was too young to mix with them, so we were only observers. Once sailors from the English Navy appeared and were easy to spot because the collars of their sailor suits were royal blue, different from the white collars of U.S. Navy sailors. We wondered why they were here. Many years later I learned that the British sailors were on our Rappahannock River in 1943 as part of the Lend-Lease program to Great Britain. They were learning how to operate American-made landing ships. Sure enough, our Rappahannock and Corotoman Rivers were playing their own remote roles in the landings of D-Day, which were to take place later in France.

Occasionally officers from the U.S. ships came ashore at the Rappahannock River Yacht Club in Irvington. Several times my dad brought two young officers home from one of the LST ships and that was how my dad's sister, Lucy, met the lieutenant who commanded the boat. She later married him. His ensign's name was Phil Young. I never forgot his name because I was in my early teens and could only secretly swoon at the sight of such a handsome fellow.

The Navy was engaged in maneuvers on the Bay, just off of the mouth of the Rappahannock and Little Bay, close to where Waterview Farm was situated on Antipoison Creek. The thunderous booms of the big guns near Waterview caused the parlor mantel mirror to fall and break, along with my much-loved mantel figurine. How fortunate we were for that to be the biggest wartime loss that we suffered. By wartime standards, that loss didn't even count.

One year during the war, at Sargent Brent's Department Store on Main Street, there was a window display of Lancaster County servicemen with their names and pictures. There was a framed picture of Paul Palmer, with a gold star that identified him as the first war casualty of the county. This "first" was quite impressive. It brought the somber reality of war close to home for all who viewed it. Later there were photos and gold stars for Garland Purcell and Chichester Pierce, who were killed at the Battle of the Bulge, and for other lost servicemen in subsequent displays.

Among others in military service whom I knew were Buddy and Billy Bussells, who lived across town in Kilmarnock. Buddy (I.M.) Bussells joined the Marines in 1943 and served in the Pacific War Theater as a scout observer at the Battle of Guam and in 1945 in the battle of Iwo Jima. He escaped injury there and was sent back to Guam in preparation for the invasion of Japan. But the atomic bombings at Hiroshima and Nagasaki, of course, ended the war before the invasion could take place. His brother, Billy (W.E. Bussells), was a heroic flyer in the Army Air Corps. He flew at Burma in Special Unit #1, flying light planes that could take supplies in and out and bring out the sick and wounded. For his bravery and daring in accomplishing these dangerous missions, he twice earned the Distinguished Flying Cross, and also the Air Medal Cluster, as well as receiving the British commendation, Mention in Despatches. Their father was a merchant marine engineering officer who was saved when his ship was sunk off of the coast of Norway. This was a local family that had all of its male members in the service of their country—as was the case in many families throughout the nation.

Nearly every family had someone who was serving in the military. Some of those in my family who served, other than my uncle Ben, were my cousins, Bob Lee Covington, Jo Beane, Billy Covington and Meredith McKenney. Meredith spent three years of his Army Air Force service in the jungles of New Guinea before finally returning home. In 1944 Bob Lee was awarded the Silver Star for gallantry in action in France when serving with the 30th Infantry, Seventh Army. He received the Purple Heart for wounds he received earlier that year. His infantry division later took Nuremberg and Munich in Germany.

In 1944, Mr. Paul Valle of Upper Lancaster County, near Mollusk, owned a large acreage of tomatoes that were ready for shipping. Due to the wartime labor force shortage he called on the local high school children to sort the tomatoes that had been picked. My class was recruited for the job and Mr. Valle provided a truck for our transportation. Away we went, gaily standing up in the truck as we rode to the spot where the tomatoes were lying on the ground in a shaded area of pine trees. We fourteen-year olds were supposed to sort the firm green fruits from those that were too ripe for shipping. When we arrived our group of boys and girls soon began a giggle-fest that developed into a tomato-tossing game by the boys. Of course, the girls didn't participate in the vigorous part of the exercise. It soon became more like a tomato ball game and was definitely out of hand when Mr. Valle appeared on the scene. He paid each of us a grand total of $1.72 wages for our day of "work" and dismissed us from his service. We became a group of subdued subjects, but were grateful not to be scolded and that we received any payment at all. It was obvious that we were not ready for steady employment.

My dad's birthday was on April 12. In 1945 Mother had planned a birthday party for him at the King Carter Tavern in Irvington, formerly the old Chesapeake Academy (later to become the Hope and Glory Inn). It was to be an especially nice supper party, as Mrs. Charlie Smith, the proprietress of the King Carter, was well known for her excellent food. The decorated cake, which mother had made, was beautiful and everything was in readiness for the party when the shocking and terrible news came at midday of President Roosevelt's sudden death in Georgia. Needless to say, a huge damper befell the birthday celebration. For days we all mourned the loss of our beloved President Franklin Roosevelt and wondered what our country would do without him.

But better news would come within the year, for the D-Day invasion in France, in June, brought a hastened end to the war in Europe in 1945 and the final victory over Japan followed in 1946.

Victory was celebrated with the ringing of church bells all over the Northern Neck and throughout the nation. There was reveling in the streets of our little towns here as in other parts of the country. At all of the community churches prayers of thankfulness were offered to God for deliverance from the war and for peace at last. Now the "lights would go on again, all over the world," just as in the lyrics of the popular wartime song.

IX

High School Days

Kilmarnock High School

In the thirties and forties public schools in the Lancaster-Northumberland County School system had no eighth grade. Therefore, when we finished seventh grade we went directly into high school.

I attended Kilmarnock High School (KHS) for two years in the new brick building on School Street in town. Mr. Henri B. Chase was the acting principal. My teachers at the school were Mary Lee Pittman (Johnson), Lucy Waring, Mrs. Helen Carter, and Rev. Jo Dameron. Miss Pittman, then a recent graduate of Mary Washington College in Fredericksburg, taught me first-year Latin grammar. She had an easygoing temperament, which encouraged our interest in the language. We received an excellent foundation in Latin from her, for which I have always been grateful. My next Latin teacher, at St. Margaret's School, said that I had the best background of any of the students she taught in her second year Latin class. This inflated my ego and I became a "standout" in Miss Trecartin's Latin class. With giddy-headed confidence I seemed to charge ahead, translating and conjugating with ease, something that was foreign to my usual nature. Miss Pittman was the real star of my Latin success.

Sports Day was held each year in May with all of the county schools in the system participating. The competitive games were primarily baseball. In conjunction with sports activities, a May Court was featured as the concluding event; it was also a competition.

Prior to May Day, a queen was elected by popular vote at each high school in the system and two attendants were selected for each of these queens. There were nine or ten high schools in the two counties, Lancaster and Northumberland, at the time. Before the May Court event took place on May Day, the reigning queen for both counties was chosen. I don't remember how this was done. This meant that her school was honored by having the reigning Queen of May Day. There was always a lot of advance speculation as to which school would have the winning May Day Queen.

The year when I was a sophomore (1946), May Day was held at KHS and it became an unusually exciting event. Most of the May Court queens and attendants were waiting upstairs in a large classroom dressed in all of their finery, just prior to making their May Court appearance outside, when suddenly a springtime storm delivered huge gusts of wind and a deluge of heavy rainfall. The surprise storm caused panic to overtake the large crowd of people that had gathered for the grand finale of the day.

Looking down out of the windows from that upstairs room we could see the crowd dashing madly for cover in all directions of the schoolyard. My eyes caught sight of the third-grade teacher from our school (the building housed both elementary grades and high school). She was running as fast as her short little legs could take her, obviously huffing and puffing her way to hurriedly reach shelter from the blast. The plump little lady was wearing what appeared to be a dark colored crepe dress. While she ran the dress rapidly crept up as it was doused with the rainwater, steadily revealing her peach-colored satin slip underneath. It looked something like a theatre curtain rising for a show and it was a very amusing sight to watch. All of the girls in the room excitedly rushed to the windows to get a view of the teacher's race in the rain. They giggled with delight and jiggled up and down on their toes at the window while they peered at the unfolding drama below. But there was also uncertainty looming in their heads as to how THIS May Day would survive the stormy catastrophe. Fortunately, only a few of the May Court girls had been caught in the downpour. They were the girls who had been first in the May Court procession outside of the building. Their dresses of net tulle were rendered limp and lifeless, producing sad-faced, teary-eyed damsels of distress. The rest of us were in luck, for we had escaped the drenching. I was one of the KHS attendants and we were wearing dresses made of yellow eyelet-embroidered cotton. Our dresses held up beautifully in the dampness when the coronation finally took place after the rains had ceased. The excitement of the day managed to erase from my memory exactly which school had won the May Queen for that year.

Once our school put on a talent show during World War II. My good friends, Jeanne Blake and Betty Jo Venable, and I decided to perform as the Andrews Sisters, singing their hit song, "Accentuate the Positive." We also sang the "G.I. Jive." As a singing trio, our at-home practice sessions provided us with plenty of giggle work. I'm not sure how well the audience received our performance on stage, but our jolly adventure in silliness made it all worth rounds of applause as far as we were concerned. After all, we were teens now!

The KHS Glee Club had an excellent choral director, Mrs. Marie Walker Kenyon, who had received her music training at Julliard Music Conservatory. She was well liked and well respected by all of the students and faculty. She had come home to live with her family in Fleet's Bay Neck while her soldier husband was overseas fighting the war. In the summer of 1945 most of our Glee Club members—about twenty boys and girls—as well as Mrs. Kenyon rode the Greyhound bus from Kilmarnock to Harrisonburg, Virginia to attend a week of music camp at Massanetta Springs. While we waited at the bus station in Harrisonburg for our transportation out to Massanetta Springs Hotel, the jukebox at the station was loudly playing music that was brand new to our ears. One of the bouncing tunes was "Boogie-Woogie" and the rhythm of the beat set some of the feet in our musical group to dancing, right there on the spot. On the same day, we also heard another new tune on the jukebox: "Sentimental Journey," by the Glenn Miller Band. That song has always caused me to reflect on our glee club trip to Massanetta Music Camp.

It was a wonderful experience to be singing with so many other young voices in a large choral group of students from all over the state. And this was in an entirely different setting: near mountains, far from our river shore. Each morning the choral sessions were held in the large, rustic, open-air auditorium that was located at the top of a rather steep hill, away from the hotel. The sound of so many voices lifting skyward out into the mountains sent a wave of tender emotions through my young frame. However, I realized that this was as close as I would ever get to attaining vocal stardom. Walking up the hill in the morning to the auditorium was something of a chore for me. I was a girl from the flat river country of our Northern Neck. But the singing that we did in the auditorium at the top of that hill made the hike, for me, worth every step upward to reach the top.

Every day we swam in the hotel pool that had the coldest water on earth, I thought. I wasn't homesick, but I preferred warm river water for my swimming. At breakfast I savored the refreshing cold taste of mountain apple juice—I usually had to have two servings. We didn't drink apple juice at home, only tomato or orange. Everything about this different environment was invigorating. I vividly remember the singing we did of "Carry Me Back to Old Virginny" and a spiritual, "Oh Lord, What a Morning." During the war, every school child learned and sang our national anthem, "The Star Spangled Banner," and the other patriotic hymns, along with the battle hymns for each of the branches of the U.S. military services. Patriotism for our country was the national spirit, which served the country well, and music played a large part in it. That music was also an important part of our Massanetta Music Camp program.

St. Margaret's School

After the war ended I had been at KHS for two years and my parents decided that I should attend St. Margaret's School in Tappahannock. Therefore, in my junior year of high school I went off to St. Margaret's to become a boarder at the all-girl Episcopal school.

I was extremely homesick for my entire first year at the school. The time between weekend or holiday visits home seemed endless to me. As I sat at my desk in the large study hall, through the riverside windows I could see cars crossing the bridge, heading homeward, and I longed to be in each one of those cars. We were allowed one weekend between September and Thanksgiving to visit home before the Christmas holiday. In the second semester we had similar weekend leave time before spring break. Adjusting to living in a four-girl room was quite a challenge. At home I had my own bedroom, my private place. The strict school rules intimidated me. I was afraid to break a single rule. Consequently, I abided by each and every rule, making myself a slave to the order. Those rules would be almost impossible for the young people of today's world to comprehend.

We were not allowed to wear lipstick until after three o'clock in the afternoon when classes ended. So our first course of action, when the bell rang to end the class day, was to race to our rooms and put on our lipstick. Ahh—this made us feel human again. I suppose the theory behind the no-class-lipstick rule was to remind us of the serious nature of academics, that lipstick was frivolous. Could that have been the reason? I never did learn the answer to that mystifying question. It seemed silly to me.

Our typical class-day routine, after classes ended, always included our afternoon getaway walk to People's Drugstore—after signing out, of course. There we could get our ice cream treats and hear music on the jukebox. I was always happy to see Mr. Rice, from home, when he came to the drugstore on his drug sales trips. He was Leon Rice's father and a very nice man. He was always especially cordial to me. Seeing him was a touch of home for me—and I loved Leon's Soda Shoppe, of course.

Chapel services were held each weekday before classes began and before study hour began in the evening. These services were held in the large study hall and always included scripture reading and singing of one or two hymns. Mrs. Elizabeth Chase, the widow of one of my dad's cousins, played the hymns on the study hall piano. She was strict and always demanded full participation in the singing. The services lasted only fifteen minutes. On Sunday we attended services at nearby St. John's Church.

Room-bell rang at 9:30 p.m., which meant that we were to be in our rooms and accounted for by a teacher who made her rounds each night on room-check duty. Lights-out was at ten o'clock, but we were allowed—after lights-out, if necessary—to go to the bathroom where lights were kept burning all night. No talking in the bathroom was permitted after ten o'clock. This meant that if you were brushing your teeth and smiled at a girl who was standing nearby, the smile was considered to be "indirect communication," for which the guilty smiler was "campused" for a week.

Everyone took all of the rules and the honor system seriously. Very few of the important rules were broken by anyone in the student body. Rarely did a student fall from grace and succumb to the disgrace of breaking the honor code for cheating, lying or stealing. If this did happen, the guilty student was summarily "shipped" from school—and that was that. She couldn't return. I remember only one incident when this happened during my two years at St. Margaret's and it caused a heavy, dark, and somber mood to fall over the entire student body.

In my first year at SMS the headmistress, Mrs. Rebecca Craighill, died suddenly after a short illness. It was the beginning of a rather low point for the school's history. She had been a strong and well-respected school administrator.

A new head of school, Miss Rebecca Brockenbrough, began her tenure in my senior year. "Miss B." was fresh out of the Women's Army Corps (WAC). She coached the hockey teams as well as administering the school according to strict guidelines, using firm discipline and giving strong punishment for any infringements.

On the hockey field—hockey was the "rah-rah" sport for S.M.S.—I was anything BUT an athlete. I hated hockey and soon discovered that I could reduce some of my gym time on the hockey field by simply being a little late for class. She ordered us to run around the periphery of the hockey field, one lap for each minute that we were late for class. I realized that by being four or five minutes late I could spend most of the game time running laps around the field. I loved it. It worked beautifully. I was secretly proud of my genius in devising such a clever solution to my athletic inadequacy.

There was very little opportunity for us to enjoy any kind of outside social experience. Each school night, following dinner, small groups of girls would gather briefly in the tiny basement radio room to dance together—jitterbugging to music playing on the record player. There were only a few who participated in this whirling activity and I always sat on the sideline to watch. I preferred to do my dancing at White Stone Beach.

Occasionally, on a Sunday afternoon, a few boys (in small groups) would come to call. Whenever they visited we were only allowed to see them by sitting in the front parlor of the main building while a teacher sat on duty at the desk in the hall, just outside of the open parlor door. There was never any danger of too much familiarity or hilarity taking place. Visits from boys were definitely discouraged.

The junior-senior prom was the only school dance of the year and the dress code rule for the dance was that students should have no bare shoulders. I remember when the skinny spinster school secretary reprimanded one girl at the prom. She marched over to the girl and tapped her on her shoulder while the couple danced and told the girl to pull up her sleeve and cover her shoulders! Humiliation was clearly not a consideration by the faculty.

In my senior year, I roomed with three good new friends that I had made. That year we were allowed to choose our roommates and I really liked my senior "roomies." Two of them were from my part of the world: Mary Lou Hinton, from Reedville, and Patsy DeHardit, from Gloucester. Madge Crawford was from Chapel Hill, North Carolina. In 1948 the student body elected Madge for May Queen and I was elected to be her maid of honor. It was a big surprise for me and I felt flattered to be chosen by my friends for this honor. My family was immensely pleased, since I had been such a homesick young thing in my junior year.

In the fall of my senior year I was called home due to my dad's sudden and very serious illness. He had suffered a massive coronary heart attack. I was out of school, at home for a week, before he was stable enough for me to return to school. His health was a condition that influenced a lot of my educational choices from that time forward. I had always been close to my dad, and wanted him to last forever.

At the end of the school year, graduation exercises were traditionally held on the riverside lawn of the main building. The platform was in place there underneath the branching limbs of a large and ancient tree. Graduation day weather was usually beautiful for the occasion. Seniors gathered on the spot in their long, white dresses carrying bouquets of flowers and blinking their eyes in the sunlight with prideful emotion and tears. On MY graduation day the rains came. Our class of twenty-three graduates in 1948 received our diplomas indoors on the stage of the dark old auditorium. This was an enormous disappointment to nearly all of the class, especially to those who were more school-spirited than I. It didn't bother me at all, exactly where the end of my high school days terminated. I only cared that graduation day had come. So it was with a big smile, and not a bit of tearful sadness, that I stepped down from the stage, diploma in hand, and tripped over the long floor-length skirt of my pretty white dress. I would be entering a new world when autumn came—I'd be going off to college at William and Mary, my dad's alma mater. I felt like a bird taking off into the great blue yonder.

Due to the rains of that day, my parents took my graduation picture the following day, in front of our home on Irvington Road in Kilmarnock. There were no other graduation photos of our class.

As time passed I came to understand the value of discipline learned by following strict rules, a strong honor system with its code of values, and the good academic background that we received at St. Margaret's. Those two years had prepared me well for new challenges that would come throughout life.

X

Down by the Riverside

In the lower Northern Neck, we rode ferryboats to cross the Rappahannock and Corotoman rivers before the Norris Bridge was built in 1957.

The Merry Point ferry, with its one- or two-car capacity, still operates from its original landing on the Corotoman River. It takes cars from the shore at Merry Point, near the village of Lancaster, to the opposite shore near Mollusk. This quaint little ferry is propelled by a motorboat that's lashed alongside the ferry. When I visited Virginia Dix

The Merry Point Ferry, 1940s. *Photo courtesy of Kilmarnock Museum.*

McGinnes in the thirties, we often crossed the Corotoman on the Merry Point ferry to take the shortcut route for getting to her home in Bertrand. Her grandmother (Dix) lived in the old house at Spring Hill Farm that was at the top of the hill above the site of the ferry landing. We occasionally went to Spring Hill when her McGinnes cousins from Washington and Florida came to visit.

A small ferryboat took traffic over the Great Wicomico River at Glebe Point until Tiper's Bridge was built there in the 1930s. A few other small ferries, like the one at Merry Point, were in operation at other locations of the Neck.

The Grey's Point toll ferry took traffic across the Rappahannock from Lancaster County to Grey's Point in Middlesex County. That ferry operated for many years from its dock in Irvington on Carter's Creek— at the old steamboat landing where Adams Floating Theatre also docked. The Irvington Beach Hotel stood at the top of the hill there, operated by the Gordon Somervells, friends of my family. This long ferry route took about forty minutes to make the crossing. The boat traveled out of Carter's Creek, then out into the river and on to Grey's Point Landing on the other side. Later the run was shortened when the ferry docked at the new White Stone landing. This new route

Miss Virginia ferryboat, photo by William Haislip. *Photo courtesy of The Rappahannock Record newspaper.*

took approximately twenty minutes. The largest ferryboat could carry probably as many as thirty vehicles. In 1957 the Norris Bridge was built across that new ferry route to Middlesex.

When the ferry was being loaded I dreaded the drive onto the boat from the wharf. I was afraid that the ferry might separate from the dock while we were driving on board. I was also uneasy about being parked at the front edge of the boat. Somehow I could never feel assured that the chocking blocks that were placed under the wheels of our car or the chain placed across the deck opening would keep the car from rolling overboard. I was a typically squeamish female.

But the moonlight trips across the river on the ferry made the crossing pleasantly romantic. Often people got out of their cars to stand by the boat's railing and watch the moonlight playing on the rippling water. The rhythmic chugging of the boat's engine motor and the strong smell of gasoline fumes vied with the luscious swishing sounds of water as the ferry carved a wake-trail gliding over the surface of the river. The moonlight's glow created a mood of rapture for the brief ride, though the odors and noises strongly conflicted with any state of bliss.

Catching the ferry was always an issue. It ran on a rigid schedule, leaving the dock on the hour from one side and on the half hour from the other. The last departure of the day was at eleven-thirty at night. If you missed the last ferry, a long distance drive around was the inevitable penalty. Many times when the ferry was pulling away from the dock, a car rushing to catch the ferry would hurriedly speed to the dock with its horn blowing, pleading for the boat to wait. On rare occasions the captain would accommodate the late arrival, but usually horn-blowing was clearly an exercise in futility. The ferry continued to motor on out into the river and the latecomer was forced to wait for the next ferry, or worse, to drive around. That long drive meant going to Tappahannock to cross the river via the Downing Bridge and then drive down to Lancaster County—a distance of forty-five miles.

Waiting at the ferry landing could sometimes be a fascinating interlude in itself. Once, on a return trip from visiting Irwin's (my husband's) family in North Carolina, just before the Norris Bridge opened in 1957, we had taken a small baby crib mattress with us for our young son, Charles, who was about six months old. Inside of our crowded car the mattress lay flat, with its two ends resting on the top edges of the car seats (the front seat and back seat). This was surely an unsafe arrangement that would never be acceptable in later years, but to our youthful way of thinking it was an okay way to do things at the time. Charles had been riding in his car seat until we arrived at Grey's Point landing, where we found that we had missed the ferry. We removed him from the car seat and young Charles spent the half hour wait at the landing crawling all over the top of the mattress. He was crawling around up high near the ceiling of the car—having a fine time indeed. It developed into a kind of merry-go-round affair and made our wait at the ferry landing very entertaining. This had occurred at the end of our long eight-hour drive from Carolina. Other people had stories of their own to tell about waiting for the ferry and some of the tales could be very choice. Perhaps some of those stories should not even be told.

After the war, when gas rationing had ended, a lot of pleasure-boating on the river was revived.

A few people operated small commercial fishing party excursions. They used deadrise motorboats to accommodate parties of about twenty people for a paid morning or evening fishing trip on the river. These were always dropline fishing trips. Winnie Abbott, of Irvington, was the most popular of the fishing party captains.

My dad kept our boat, the *Nanbec*, docked in Irvington. We had many picnics with family and friends aboard when we went dropline fishing in the river. We always headed for the "best spot" (fishing grounds), which was located opposite the high bank on the shore where the old "Pop Castle" house still stands. There were usually throngs of boats anchored there, fishing for the plentiful spot, croaker, perch, shad (in season), flounder and bluefish. Sugartoads and eels often came up on our lines from the deep as well. Many times Dad entertained groups of his insurance associates from Richmond for a day of river fishing. That was a big treat for those city fellows and a jolly time was always had by all. In the fall of the year, my dad enjoyed trolling for rockfish. This was strictly a man's sport and the ladies were never on those trips.

The river and its tributaries also provided shorelines for a lot of duck and goose hunting. In the early days (thirties and forties) it was not uncommon for Daddy and others to bag nearly fifty of the birds on one hunting expedition. This was the legal limit set at that period of time. There was one black lady, who lived down on Waverly Avenue in Kilmarnock, who picked and dressed all of the hundreds of ducks that were brought to her by the large number of duck hunters in the area. It was hard for people to imagine how she could accomplish such a feat or what her life must have been like, yet she was always agreeable and never refused to accept the jobs that were brought to her.

Sailboating was also a popular river sport, of course. One summer day, when I was about fifteen, I went sailing with one of my friends, Lee Liggan, Jr., who had a Snipe sailboat, the *Dinky-Do*. We were well out into the river when Charlie Somervell came alongside our boat in his Snipe, the *Baby Face*. Virginia Harvey, a girlfriend, was riding with him. An idea came into the boys' heads for the girls to switch places and ride in the other boat. I was to get into the *Baby Face* first, so my transfer began there in the middle of the river. As I cautiously arose and began to step from one boat to the other, the boom of one of the boats swung around and knocked me overboard between the two boats. When I surfaced from the dunking, both of the boys were yelling and arguing with each other as to whose fault it was. But neither of them seemed concerned about how or where I was, there in the middle of the river, between two boats. I finally called out to them, "Hey, how about me?" I needed to catch their attention for the boys to take some action to start getting me back aboard a boat. None of us were wearing life preservers—after all, we were "river ducks" who swam like fish, so worry about drowning would not occur to any of our crowd. We had fun laughing about the incident afterward. I guess Lady Luck might've also been sailing along with us, or with me, on that day.

The Rappahannock River Yacht Club on Carter's Creek in Irvington was the place where not only adults, but young people too, could socialize and enjoy boating and other activities. In the nineteen forties we teenagers whose families were members of the club had several parties there, in both winter and summertime. We always danced to the jukebox music of the Big Bands. "Jitterbugging" was the dance style of the time. It was customary for a boy to "break" on a dancing couple by tapping on the male's shoulder so that he could be the girl's new partner for a few dance steps, at least until another boy came to break in and claim rights to dance with the girl. Girls were often flattered by the number of different dance partners they collected by getting breaks. They could also be very unhappy by getting "stuck" too long with an undesirable partner (unattractive or a bad dancer). This was not a new custom, but the whirl of jitterbugging only made it more exciting for our age group.

One summer our small group of girls gave a formal dance at the yacht club and we spent most of the summer planning for it. We met each week at one of our homes to plan our invitation list, food, decorations, and the jukebox tunes that we could special order from the Harveys, who were in that kind of business. The planning sessions were almost as much fun as the actual dance. Our parents, of course, were the chaperones for the party. Dressing in formal dresses made it a very special affair. The jukebox was inside the small clubhouse and we danced there as well as outside on the large screened porch. We served punch and some soft drinks, along with a lot of olive sandwiches, Vienna sausage snacks and cheeses with Ritz crackers. They were the choices of party fare for us and no thought of alcoholic beverages entered our heads in our high school years. Our decorations were colorful crepe paper streamers that we hung from the ceiling of the main room, but by evening the damp river breeze had caused them to sag to the floor. So upon arrival for the party we had to remove all of our decorations that had looked so fine and had been so much fun to hang. However, such a small tragedy did nothing to dampen the spirits of anyone. The dance was a highlight of our summer.

For almost a week of one summer in the thirties (or early forties) people in this area were drawn, at nighttime, to Carter's Creek and the Rappahannock River to observe the waters there. The best viewing spot was in Carter's Creek where the water seemed to glow with light coming from below the entire surface of the creek. The unusual occurrence was said to be due to a kind of phosphorus buildup and was the only time that such a phenomenon had been observed in these waters. It was quite an eerie spectacle and caused much talk throughout the area.

The yacht club in Irvington was the site of the Virginia Sailing Regatta for several years in the late forties and early fifties. In other years the event took place in Gloucester and also in Norfolk at the Norfolk Yacht and Country Club. Sailboats participated from yacht clubs up and down the Virginia coastline. It was a very large event with hundreds of boats sailing on the Rappahannock. When the regatta was held at Irvington, boats docked at the RRYC or moored in Carter's Creek. Classes of sailboats in the races ranged from the smallest Penguin class, to the mid-sized Snipes and the larger Hamptons. There were no large yachts in these races.

Penguins racing on Carter's Creek at the Virginia Sailing Regatta at RRYC, 1945.

In July of 1946 a small group from RRYC went to Norfolk to take part in the Virginia Sailing Regatta. This was a very unique trip—great fun and a very memorable adventure. Two of the boys, Lee Liggan and Charlie Somervell, were entering the races with their boats in the Snipe class. Tom McGinnes provided his large buy-boat, the *Julian*, for transporting the boys with their sailboats, their crews, and their parents to the races, along with three of my girlfriends and our parents. There were about twenty-five people aboard, including the boat captain.

We left at eleven o'clock on that moonlit night from the yacht club dock in Irvington. We all gathered on the boat's deck, where the two sailboats were stored, to make the overnight trip. The boat made its way out of the creek and into the river, then out into the Chesapeake and continued down the Bay, reaching Norfolk around sunrise. We managed to catch a few catnaps as we lay on blankets spread out on the deck, but we spent most of the night singing and gazing at the starry sky with the moonlight shining on the waters of the Bay, enjoying the exhilarating thrill of this adventure. Needless to say, we were not a very alert group when we arrived in Norfolk, but youth seemed to carry everyone through, including our parents, without any ill effects. The *Baby Face*, Charlie's boat, placed on top in winning Snipe class awards. It was a beautiful shade of bright green, a shiny and sleek little gem of a boat, and Charlie was an excellent sailor. His dad, Gordon Somervell, an avid boater himself, was always very proud of Charlie's accomplishments in the *Baby Face*.

White Stone Beach was the legendary place of summer fun for the lower Northern Neck. It played a large part in the lives of many people in the area who cherish their memories of the place.

The pavilion building, a former tomato canning house, was situated beside the site of the dock at the old Taft P.O. and store, where steamboats had stopped until 1930. It was at the bottom of a hill where sandy beaches stretched along the shoreline. The Culver family bought the old cannery building in 1916 and transformed it into a resort/amusement facility by

White Stone Beach days.

renovating the cannery building and adding a dining room and riverside cottages. They operated it throughout the twenties, thirties, and on into the seventies, when the Beach finally succumbed to the social changes of the sixties and seventies. The Beach season ran each year from May until sometime in September.

The pavilion had a dance floor and soda fountain inside, with an open porch over the water on the outside. A long wharf extended from the porch into the river with a netted swimming area adjoining it. The row of cottage rooms was built along one end of the pavilion, on the side toward the old Taft fish factory that was located down on the western shore. The dining room was adjacent to the large covered porch on the other side of the building.

No better homecooked meals could be found anywhere than those prepared in Amy Culver's Beach kitchen. Her soft shell crabs were a specialty of the house. They were always the small, tender crabs, never large, tough or tasteless. In the early evening we could sit at the dinner table in the Beach's quiet dining room and hear the gentle sounds of river water lapping at the pilings underneath the floor. It was a lazy rhythm heard in the stillness of the room and it produced a mild drifting sensation in our heads. Gentle river breezes blew in through the open windows while the golden glow of an early summer evening added another dimension to the idyllic rustic setting. It became a treasured memory of a simpler time and place.

Whenever I approached the Beach, as I rode down the hill my senses were immediately invigorated when I caught the first whiffs of salty air that emanated from the river. Just as the old Taft Store, the dining room, and then the pavilion came into view I always felt a sharp jolt of eagerness to run and jump into the water, or to hurry to rush out onto the dance floor for an afternoon of jitterbugging to jukebox tunes. Whether I rode in a car or pedaled a bicycle down that hill, the sensation was always the same for me. It never changed.

Entering the pavilion we were met with pungent salty river wind that was always blowing into the building through the large open window spaces. As children, after we finished our swimming for the day, Gilbert Culver, his mother, or his wife, Amy, would serve us ice cream cones or icy slush drinks from behind the big marble fountain. There were often several men sitting on stools at the far side of the counter drinking an afternoon beer. They were quiet, never rowdy, and there were only a few of these fellows who came during the day. They liked to play games on the two pinball machines that were in the pavilion.

"Pop" Culver, Gilbert's father, usually sat on the front porch, legs crossed, rocking in his chair while he puffed on his cigar. His necktie always hung around his neck, though it was never tied, and he always wore suspenders to support his trousers. Pop Culver might well have purposely stationed himself there as a sentinel, for he frequently raised his voice in disciplinary yells to any unruly behavior that was taking place by the swimmers on the wharf or in the water. There was no lifeguard on duty and swimmers dashed up and down the wharf excitedly jumping into the water or sliding down the wide old wooden sliding board.

That sliding board was a phenomenal feature of the Beach swimming experience because not one person was ever known to get a fanny splinter from sliding down its wet-down surface. Many years later, Bernice Culver (Shelly), Amy and Gilbert's daughter, told me that early each season the sliding board was coated with an unknown treatment to insure that the board was tightly sealed. Ahh—the mystery has finally been solved!

Our bunch on the dock at White Stone Beach: (left to right) Jean W., Jeanne B., Betty Jo V., me, and Grace Ann S.

Fish netting was strung between fish-stake poles in the water, outlining a large area that served as a supposed barrier from stinging nettles. This area ran from the shallow-water end of the wharf, near the sliding board, out to the deep-water end of the wharf where there was a wooden diving board. Throughout nearly all of the 1940s there were still no freshwater swimming pools in the area.

There was another important feature of the great times that everyone had at White Stone Beach: that, of course, was the Saturday night dances. The large square dance floor was in the center of the pavilion. It was raised so that one step up put you onto the dance floor. There was a small orchestra space located at one front corner of the square and the jukebox sat next to the band space with the piano permanently in place nearby. An open fence railing bordered the entire dance floor with rows of benches placed behind the railing. This created a viewing gallery for onlookers. There were plenty of curiosity seekers who took their seats to watch and be entertained. A few tables with benches were outside, at the front side of the dance floor for those who sat to drink soft drinks or beer, which were the only beverages served at the Beach.

On Saturday nights people of all types came for the big dance of the summer week. The music started at nine o'clock and ended promptly at midnight, which signaled the end of the dance. In the forties and fifties the live music for the dances was usually provided by "Junior" Harvey's local band and sometimes by Gippy Smith's Richmond band. In later years (late fifties and sixties) The Dynatones played for the dances, but that came after our crowd had grown away from the Beach scene.

On the well-lighted waterfront porch of the pavilion there were a few small ice cream parlor tables where people sat with their friends. During my college years, on most Saturday nights a group of us liked to gather at a front corner space on the porch. We arranged several of the round tables in a grouping near the waterside edge of the porch, close to the dining room wall. Our crowd stayed close together, apart from the rest of the mob, and made our own fun. Occasionally a fight broke out near the front entrance and the troublemakers were quietly escorted away by the sheriff's department. This seemed like a remote happening to us because we were always sitting on the opposite side of the pavilion, away from any of that kind of activity. We were usually unaware of the events that were taking place on the other side of the building. Often there was "booze" drinking being done by a few people outside in the parking lot, but amazingly, not a great deal of it. White Stone Beach was never known as the "rowdy" beach of the Northern Neck. It had a reputation for fun without trouble.

For several years after the Beach had closed, it lay idle, cradling memories of a time that had been lost forever. The Culver family graciously allowed the Grace Episcopal Church women to use the old empty pavilion as the site for a huge and very successful September sale in the 1970s. Antiques were auctioned, and used clothing (dubbed "Fractured Fashions" by the church ladies), "white elephant" items, and Brunswick stew (from my mother's own famous recipe) were sold. People came from all over the Northern Neck, including some political figures from Richmond and Westmoreland counties. It was the "last hurrah" for White Stone Beach. That sale day had been a reunion for many people—a chance to revisit the hallowed place of so many memories. Some time later all of the Beach buildings were destroyed by a planned fire that erased any signs that the resort of a former era had ever existed at the site.

The black community had its own popular dance hall that was located just outside of Kilmarnock, at the foot of the hill, near the Boys' Camp Road on Route 3. It was a lively entertainment spot on Saturday nights, all during the year, though it was not on the river. It was known as Simon Conquest's place.

Breezy Cove was the name our family gave to our cottage on Antipoison Creek. It had formerly been the tenant house on Waterview Farm. After the war ended and the family had sold Waterview, my dad decided to remodel the old tenant house for a summer cottage. We could spend the summer on the water and he could be away from the telephone that often rang with business calls at home in Kilmarnock. We never installed a phone at the cottage for that reason. Before my dad's death we spent several summers there, having wonderful times—with a constant flow of relatives and friends. Across the cove were the Bullards, from Richmond, who had bought Waterview. They painted the house pink. It was a summer home for them and they renamed it "Bay Hall." Nanee (my grandmother) had a hard time seeing the family home painted that color, but she never said a word—only shook her head and looked away whenever it was mentioned. The Henry B. Smiths, of Petersburg, spent summers nearby on the creek.

They had moved one of the Waterview farm buildings to a nearby spot on the creek and made additions that transformed it into a cottage for them. I had some William and Mary friends and others for house parties at Breezy Cove and my cousin Gerry spent a lot of time with us there as well. Daddy always reserved one long weekend of the season for Nanee and Corie to visit us on the creek. Nanee could be close to her old home that way.

After my dad's heart attack, he was not allowed to handle a larger boat like our cabin cruiser, *Nanbec II,* had been, so he got a neat little Chris-Craft speedboat and we had great fun zooming around in it. The boat had a sleek mahogany hull and red leather seats. There were no more fishing expeditions, but we had a different kind of fun anyway.

Mother went to a country auction sale that was held nearby and found a crude old table that was covered on top with linoleum floor covering. She paid fifty cents for it. We used it in our rudimentary big square kitchen at the cottage. It was perfect for us to use for seating a lot of people at the table, cottage style. That was where we picked and ate our steamed hard crabs. Often we were barefoot at the cottage and once, when we were steaming hard crabs, some of the crabs managed to get out of the pot and

Daddy and Mother in the *Nanbec III,* leaving our dock at Breezy Cove.

crawl around on the kitchen floor. We had to be quick to avoid the grip of a crab claw on our feet. It caused us to do some wild dancing in the kitchen that day. What fun times we did have!

We used our small wooden skiff boat for catching crabs. I often poled around the edge of the cove in the evening, but seldom in the early morning, to try to catch a few soft crabs with my crab net. I was never good at this sport. Those soft crabs were simply too clever at hiding on the murky creek bottom. They were fast and elusive whenever their big old eyes spotted the crab net hovering over them and they quickly scooted to bury themselves in the mud. The evening hours of poling around the cove's shoreline was a relaxing time to savor the tranquility of the creek setting. An occasional squawk from a seagull flying overhead was the only interrupter of the quiet surroundings. I loved all of this and carefully tucked it away in my head with all of my treasured creek memories.

At the end of summer in 1946 my parents arranged to have a sixteenth birthday party for me. They obtained the use of the *Julian* from their friend, Tom McGinnes (Virginia Dix's dad), who owned the buyboat for some of his seafood enterprises. It was the same boat that was used for the Norfolk trip to the sailing regatta. They invited about thirty-five of my friends for a cruise on the *Julian* to The Cowshed at Millenbeck, on the Corotoman River. We left the dock at the yacht club in the late afternoon and motored out into the Rappahannock, then into the Corotoman River to land at The Cowshed dock. There was a netted-in swimming area on the shore where we could swim. This was a private party, so we had the dance hall facility all to ourselves for a picnic and dancing. The log-cabin-style Cowshed had an upstairs balcony that encircled the dance floor below. Along with other tunes, the jukebox blasted out "The Beer Barrel Polka," playing it repeatedly for our evening of fun. Jackie (my old playmate) and I whirled around the balcony numbers of times, dancing a polka step until we fell to the floor from sheer exhaustion. The tune was drumming on and on about beer, but there was only Coca-Cola being consumed by this crowd. It was the beverage of our age group and it filled us with as much joy as any "Kickapoo Joy Juice" could ever produce. We had the time of our lives dancing and laughing together. This was the beautiful era of fun and frolic for young people, without any remote thoughts of cigarettes, alcohol, or drugs.

The Cow Shed dance hall at Millenbeck, site of my birthday party.

My dad was a fun-loving person who was as "pleased as punch" to see that his daughter's sixteenth birthday was such a resounding success. It was the only time any of our crowd went to The Cowshed. We were, after all, White Stone Beachers.

In the fifties some of us began to gravitate to The Tides Inn's saltwater swimming pool. On Saturday nights, small crowds of local young adults sometimes danced under the stars around the perimeter of the pool and later, in the Bubble House there at poolside. Times were changing and we had grown a bit more sophisticated. That pool, located beside the waters of Carter's Creek, enabled us to continue basking in our charmed river life experience, while it was beginning to broaden to a new horizon. We were proud that one of our own native sons had created this luxurious resort. It has always been true that native Northern Neckers have a strong appreciation for the good life that this special place can afford.

In 1956 Indian Creek Yacht and Country Club was organized by a group of local businessmen, along with a Richmond developer. It brought another dimension to our life on the river. This gave us another swimming pool in the area and also a larger golf course than the first small one, which was at The Tides Inn at that time.

A public swimming pool had been opened in Fleet's Bay Neck. It was called The Tidewater Recreation Center. However, the facility only operated for a few years.

XI

College Times

Leaving for college in Williamsburg in the fall of 1948, I was typical of many Northern Neck natives who chose to attend William and Mary. It was the second oldest college in the country, had a fine academic reputation, and Lancaster County's own Robert "King" Carter had once served on its board. Both my dad and his father were alumni of the college. Those facts plus its close proximity to home all made it the perfect college choice for me. Admittedly though, I was ready for a coeducational environment after spending two years at an all-girl boarding school.

Following the wonderful summertime at home it was hard to leave these shores for the winter months of school, yet I was anxious to begin the year in college. Once a couple of us raced back home from Williamsburg after we had registered for our fall classes in order to spend the last weekend of summer on the river before classes began. On that race down the hill to catch the ferry we were lucky to arrive in time to be the last car to get on board. We didn't have to lose any of our precious weekend time at home waiting at the ferry dock to cross the river.

There were plenty of familiar people at William & Mary when I was there. Gayle Ruffin was my sophomore year roommate. She and I had become great friends at St. Margaret's. One of my Irvington friends, Charlie Somervell, was a Kappa Alpha brother of "Hop" (John H.) Harding, of Northumberland County. Jack Hughes was a Pi Kappa Alpha at the college, which pleased me a lot. ΠΚΑ had been my dad's fraternity and Jackie had been my childhood playmate. There were several others from the Neck at W&M at the same time I was there. Wendell Haynie, Howard Straughan, and Betty Jo Venable entered in the same year and Ebbie Shelton was a sophomore. Hugh Haynie, of Reedville, was a ΠΚΑ and after college became a noted political cartoonist.

At that point in time, dating at home in the lower Neck usually meant going to see a movie at the Fairfax or the Lee theater in White Stone. Occasionally we drove to Tappahannock to see a movie at the Daw theater. For several years there was a small gathering place called "The Juke Box," between Irvington and Kilmarnock, where we could dance to jukebox music during the winter months. It was a popular spot until it burned in the mid 1950s. We always had plenty of things to do or places to go.

Of course, summertime dances were always held on Saturday night at White Stone Beach—THE capital spot for everyone's summer fun. At Christmastime we attended the Holly Ball, of course, or drove as far as Hague, in Westmoreland County, for the annual Christmas night dance; to Heathsville, in Northumberland County, for the "Snow Ball"; and once to Warsaw for a dance when the nationally popular Raph Flanaggan Band played there. The fathers of the boys that we dated were trusting parents who gave their sons the use of the family car for a long evening of driving when there was very little traffic on the rural highways. Few drank anything alcoholic, other than beer, and they were usually fairly responsible drivers. The girls were primarily Coca-Cola drinkers, though other spirits were a part of the scene to some degree. Drugs were simply unheard of, a total non-issue at the time. Some girls smoked cigarettes, but I never did. I always hated the idea. I guess that my grandfather's cigar smoking had caused some of my disdain for smoking-related pastimes. But it was more likely because my dad's heart attack had been a warning against smoking and anything that could be hurtful to his health influenced my own choices.

In December of 1950 the first Christmas Assembly (later termed, "Tidewater Assembly") was held at The Tides Inn. It was the first debutante presentation to be held in the Northern Neck. There were seventeen of us presented, though all were not in their freshman year of college for this first Assembly presentation. It was a charity ball and a buffet dinner was served to the throng of people at the affair. The hotel guests had left at the end of the summer season, so the Inn was packed to capacity for the event with Assembly guests. Debutantes with their escorts, their families, committee members, and patrons of the newly formed Tidewater Foundation all gathered there for the affair.

The age-old Holly Ball had been rejuvenated after its suspension during the wartime years and was being held in the Kilmarnock High

School auditorium at that time. The Holly Ball of the Northern Neck had begun in 1895. Its custom of crowning a "Queen of the Holly Realm," elected by popular votes cast by the gentlemen at the ball, continues today. It was not originally a debutante ball. Later, in 1958, the Christmas Tidewater Assembly merged with the Holly Ball and the queen's election format changed significantly.

In 1950 the traditional coronation of a Holly Queen took place at the old Ball and that evening I became the much-surprised, newly elected Holly Ball Queen. An old Northern Neck friend of mine, Wayland A. ("Bud") Doggett, was my date for the Ball and therefore served as my Minister to the Queen. My dad was unable to be at either the Christmas Assembly or the Holly Ball that year. He was at home in bed, suffering with the recurrence of his heart condition.

Photo Courtesy Richmond Times-Dispatch

Senator R. O. Norris, Jr., of Lively, places the crown on the head of Holly Festival Queen, Miss Nancy Hubbard, at the Holly Ball held in Kilmarnock Wednesday evening, December 27. Whayland Doggett, of Heathsville, Minister to the Queen, looks on.

Holly Ball news clip, 1950.

In my junior year of college I transferred from William and Mary to Richmond Professional Institute (later to become Virginia Commonwealth University) to attend the School of Design there. It was a full three-year program that was recognized as one of the best in the country. Although I was not a great artist, I did have an affinity for the design arts. In the fifties, females who received their liberal arts degrees usually chose to become schoolteachers or social workers, and neither appealed to me. I was dead set against it.

At RPI there were many Northern Neck friends of mine. Bobby (Robert Carter) Ball was in my design department classes; Virginia

Harvey, Mary Tayloe Murphy, Mariah Biddlecomb, and Suzanne Gardiner were all in my dormitory on Park Avenue; and one year Barbara Reamy was my roommate. Alex Fleet and "Bud" (Wayland) Doggett were also on campus.

Her Royal Highness
Queen Nancy
Empress of the Holly Realm
requests the presence of
Her Royal Subjects
at the
Holly Festival
to be held in the Castle at Kilmarnock
on the evening of
Wednesday, December Twenty-sixth
nineteen hundred fifty-one
at ten o'clock
Wayland A. Doggett
MINISTER TO THE QUEEN

In January of 1951, right after the eventful and exciting 1950 Christmas holiday during my second year at RPI, I came home from school for the weekend, traveling with someone who had given me a ride from Richmond. During those days few college students owned cars and we traveled with people who could take us to our destinations, unless we rode the Greyhound bus. The

Holly Ball invitation issued in my name, as the retiring queen, 1951.

identity of the person who had given me a ride for that trip home has forever afterward remained a blank in my mind, due to the shock I received on that fateful day. To my horror, when we arrived at home I was met with the unbelievable news that Daddy had passed away shortly before we drove into the yard. Mother had been preparing to take him for a drive when he collapsed at the front door. He was forty-seven years old. The shock and grief soon began to affect choices I made about my education.

My dad had been a very popular fellow in the community. He had a very outgoing personality, loved all kinds of people, and had worked hard to build his business from scratch, during the Depression and War years, into a strong and successful one. He served on the Kilmarnock Town Council from 1942-50 and was on the vestry of Grace Church for many years, as well as on the board of directors of the Virginia Association of Insurance Agents. People respected his business capabilities and he looked out for many people, in a business way, who were experiencing hard times during the Depression. My dad's death changed life in many ways for

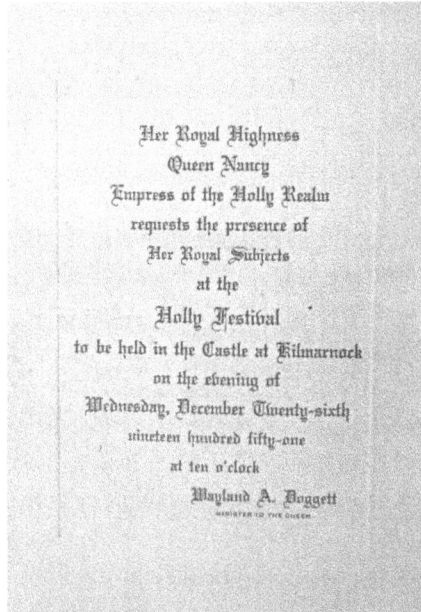

Mother and me.

After mother became a widow, Aunt Celeste began spending winters with her, since both were now widows. Gerry was away at Christchurch School in Middlesex County.

On March 17, 1952, I was at home on spring break from college. Shortly after 2 a.m., we were awakened by relentless blasts of the town fire alarm siren. When we looked out of our window into the night, the awesome blaze of fire that we saw in the sky appeared to be as gigantic as the sight we had recently seen of Rome burning in the movie *Quo Vadis*. The town was on fire! This was the third town fire that Kilmarnock had experienced and it raged all night, until dawn, before it could be controlled. In the early morning the three of us joined many other ladies in town to cook breakfast in the new Grace Church parish house for the weary volunteer firemen who had come from all over the Neck to help save the town.

As the fire burned throughout the night, my uncle, Ben, who had joined Dad's insurance agency, and Jim Kirk, another fellow who worked there at the time, frantically hurried to retrieve all of the business files from the office, which was then located on Waverly Avenue. They feared that the fire would surely also engulf that end of town. It was an unusually windy March night and the windswept fire appeared to be an unstoppable inferno. Due to the outpouring of help from the volunteer fire departments from almost every town in the Neck and as far away as Warsaw, the town was saved. Most of the businesses in the north end of town were the only ones that were destroyed.

The fire had started in the old Hazel Building—where the Opera House, upstairs, had once been the scene of dancing school revues. People speculated that the origin of the fire might have been a carelessly tossed cigarette—tossed by someone who was staying in the hotel section of the large, rambling, barn-like structure. The high winds caused the fire to leap across the street and ignite the awnings that were on buildings all along the opposite side. Leon Rice's Soda Shoppe was one of the first to be set aflame by the gusty winds of that St. Patrick's Day fire. The shop had stood almost directly across from the Hazel building and in only a few minutes it was swallowed up by the wildfire. On the same side of the street, Sargent's Department Store was next to Rice's, at the corner of

Main and Church streets. The inferno quickly swamped it and raced along the entire length of the block on that side of the street, destroying each of the tall cinderblock store buildings as far down the street as the Masonic building, where the fire was finally stopped.

In order to reestablish commercial activity at the north end of town, new buildings were soon constructed. The simple design of these one-story brick buildings reflected the haste in which they were built.

Only seven months after the disastrous town fire, in October, the county observed its tricentennial of the founding of Lancaster County in 1652. The two-day celebration brought hundreds of people to the county. Most of the planning for the affair was done by local county historians: Mrs. C. T. (Bessie) Pierce and Mrs. T. D. (Aileen) McGinnes, assisted by Mrs. Willis S. (Norinne) Bryant, Mrs. Robert Y. Barkley, and Mrs. T. Welby (Bertha) Bonner. These were all very active ladies of the Lancaster County Women's Club.

The celebration opened on the grounds of Kilmarnock High School with the coronation of Queen Lancaster, my old friend, Virginia Dix McGinnes. She was crowned by Governor John S. Battle who delivered a speech amidst much pomp and ceremony. Jesse Ball DuPont appeared as a distinguished guest representing one of the oldest families in the county.

At Lancaster there was the dedication of a plaque honoring Lancaster County veterans of World War I, with music by the Langley Air Force band.

A Grande Parade took place during the afternoon. It included numerous floats depicting historical county sights, local fire departments, businesses, and the combined Lancaster County school bands. The Queen's Court rode in the parade on flatbed trucks. Members of the court were: the queen, the prelate, a crown bearer, train bearers, trumpeters, flower girls, pages, princesses (from several other Virginia counties), and eight Lancaster County maids. I remember riding on the truck with the maids in the queen's court on that uncomfortable journey of many miles through the county. The parade began at White Stone and ended beyond the village of Lively. In the evening an elaborate outdoor drama, "The Pageant," was presented at Kilmarnock High School. It featured many local amateur actors portraying fourteen scenes of county history. It was, indeed, a very lengthy performance.

On the second day there were tours of the old buildings in Lancaster. The entire village was temporarily closed to traffic and people rode buses into the village from distant parking locations. Dr. Francis P. Gaines, president of Washington and Lee University, made an address from the new brick steps of the old Lancaster jail where a temporary stage had been erected. Then several scenes of the historical pageant were presented while the audience viewed the spectacle sitting in chairs on the village green. In the evening the Pageant was again performed in its entirety, outdoors at Kilmarnock High School. Finally, to close the two-day event a Queen's Ball was held inside of the school – with music by the Claude Thornehill Orchestra.

The Tricentennial Celebration was truly a BIG EVENT in the annals of Lancaster County history.

XII

Changing Places

After college I spent part of a summer on a student tour of Europe with two of my William and Mary sorority (KAΘ) friends, Mary Ellen McCloskey and Becky Smith. The hometown part of my trip was in winning the big prize drawing of the Kilmarnock Firemen's Carnival. While I was away on my trip Mother had bought tickets for the drawing, in my name, and my ticket was drawn from the barrel, making me the lucky winner of a television set. In 1953 television was new in the scheme of things and not everyone owned a set. This big surprise upon my return home served as a reminder that no matter how far away, my family and hometown were always near and dear to my heart.

Following that summer I found a job in Richmond, just as many of us from this area did. There were very few job opportunities here, so after completing high school or college many people migrated to other parts of the country.

Part of the time while working there, I lived outside of the city with the family of my friend, Gayle Ruffin, at Upper Marlbourne Farm, close to Mechanicsville. It was nice to be in the country, a bit closer to the Northern Neck. By that time I had a car and could drive into the city to my job in the plant records department of C&P Telephone Co., working on maps. Several girls from RPI art departments were working there.

While working in Richmond, I also lived in the city for a while, where I met my future husband, Irwin Clark. He was from North Carolina and a very "Southern gentleman" type. Irwin was with the Army Counter Intelligence Corps (CIC) and was sent to Richmond, instead of to Germany, following a serious illness that he suffered upon completion of Intelligence School training at Ft. Hollabird, Maryland.

When we were married, in June of 1955, our wedding took place at Christ Church, where my grandparents had been married in June of

Irwin and me on our wedding day at Christ Church, 1955.

1902. Gayle Ruffin was my maid of honor and my bridesmaids were Jeanne Blake (my early best friend); Mary Ellen McCloskey (my William & Mary friend); and Frances Chase, one of my cousins. The little flower girls were my young first cousins, Ann Carter Green and Anne Crawford Hubbard. My uncle, Ben (Dad's brother), gave me away and Gene Covington, my cousin Bob Lee Covington's wife, sang a solo for the ceremony. Our wedding was one of only a few that had been held in the old church since the days of Nanee's wedding.

Irwin's groomsmen were his North Carolina high school friends: Claude S. ("Pot") Burton and Steve Hamlet; his Davidson College schoolmate, G. Irvin Richardson; a UNC friend, Edwin Pate; and one of his CIC service buddies, Gerry Tjoflat. Irwin's father suffered a mild stroke on the way to Virginia for the wedding and was hospitalized in Winston-Salem and unable to "stand up" for his son, therefore, Irwin's cousin, Lauder Gibson, acted as best man and the wedding did take place as planned. On the day before the wedding, however, we had been afraid that all plans might have to be changed.

We had the reception at The Tides Inn. Big Steve, Mother's relative who owned the Inn, had been anxious for us to have our wedding reception there. All went well, with my only regret being that my dad was not there to share my special day. He would have been very pleased with my groom.

After our wedding Irwin and I moved to Laurinburg, North Carolina, where he joined the textile mills that were owned by his mother's relatives.

There in Scotland County nearly everyone was of Scottish descent and, naturally, Presbyterian, as Irwin was, although his great grandfather (being of Welsh descent) had founded the small Episcopal church (St. David's) in the town. Laurinburg was a very nice Southern town. Its streets were lined with large old oak trees and its people were warm and friendly, and very strong Presbyterians.

However, we didn't stay away from the Northern Neck for very long.

XIII

Happy Returns

The call of Virginia beckoned, so Irwin and I soon came back to Kilmarnock. If we had stayed in North Carolina, he was to be sent to the New York sales office of Morgan-Jones textile mills and we both preferred small town life. My uncle Ben needed another man in the insurance office and Irwin was accustomed to small town life. He had grown up in Reidsville, North Carolina, near Danville, Virginia, where his father had been employed in the tobacco industry. So we returned to Kilmarnock and began our life together here in the Northern Neck.

It was good to be back and we were definitely in a small town in the country. Upon our return, Irwin joined our family insurance office, Hubbard Insurance Agency, and he soon became recognized for his competence as a businessman. He joined the Episcopal church with me, harking back to his own Episcopalian roots. As time passed he became active in Grace Church Sunday school, served on the vestry of the church, and became a trustee of old Christ Church, where we had been married. He also served on the boards of several community institutions and was active in community organizations and other activities. After Ben's death Irwin became president and managing officer of the insurance agency.

In 1956 and early in 1957, we started our family with the birth of our two sons. There were no hospitals here, so both of them were born in Richmond. Many local mothers were rushed, in labor, to a Richmond hospital for the birth of a child. They can recall the nervous anxiety that they experienced on that eighty-mile trip to Richmond via the long winding route to cross the bridge at Tappahannock, and then the long remaining miles to reach the hospital in Richmond. My trips for childbirth were the same. On rare occasions the trip was not completed before a child was born en route. One friend of ours got only as far as Nuttsville, near Lively, before her son was born at the country home/office of Dr. C. T. Pierce. When our daughter was born, after the Norris Bridge had opened, we still had to make the trip to Richmond for her birth in a hospital, since there still was no hospital in the area in 1965.

The Lancaster County Junior Women's Club was active in the 1950s. It provided the younger women, such as me, with an outlet for community involvement. Other women's organizations at the time were the Lancaster County Women's Club; the Kilmarnock and Chesapeake Bay garden clubs; the White Stone Women's Club; the Order of the Eastern Star; and the Holly Ball Committee, along with the Tidewater Foundation. I served on the Holly Ball Committee for several years and, as historian, authored its centennial year history of the Ball.

Men's organizations of the time were the Kilmarnock-Irvington-White Stone Rotary Club; the Lancaster County Lions Club; the Masonic Order; and the Upper Lancaster Ruritan Club.

The Lancaster County Lions produced a minstrel show each spring for a few years during the fifties. It was primarily a musical show with club members providing the talent. The event was very popular and attracted large crowds at the Kilmarnock High School auditorium.

The social life of the area was dominated by the Holly Ball that had begun in 1895, followed by the Christmas Tidewater Assembly that originated in 1950. The Northern Neck Assembly was organized in the 1950s. The cotillion was made up of young couples from all over the Northern Neck. Dinner-dances were held twice each year, rotating from the upper to the lower Northern Neck to locations where the private dances were held. It was exclusively a social affair, never a charity function.

Boy and Girl Scout troops and Little League football and softball were outstanding youth activities in the community, outside of school sports. Our children were all involved in these and I was a Cub Scout den mother for a few years.

In the 1950s the Tidewater Foundation provided funding for operation of a public swimming pool located in Fleet's Bay Neck, outside of Kilmarnock. It was the first public swimming pool in the area and, for a short time, was a popular place for many people. Swim lessons were conducted there by the Red Cross. Swimming lessons were also given at White Stone Beach by the Red Cross.

This area was a safe and wholesome environment for rearing children. Life seemed busy, but definitely moved at a relaxed tempo. Very few people were getting rich, but life here was, indeed, sweet and simple. We loved it that way. There were, however, shortfalls in our idyllic setting that needed improvement. These included the need for better schools, a hospital, nursing care facilities, and a public library.

Running off to the city to shop would be a continuing custom, but new shops were bringing more variety and convenience closer to home. Kilmarnock had always been the commercial hub for the lower Northern Neck and the town continued to develop along that course.

XIV
Crossing Over

With the opening of the Norris Bridge, we were no longer cut off from the mainland at the end of the long peninsula between the Rappahannock and Potomac rivers. A land of promise had been opened for new people to develop and enjoy. This new venue would soon become known by newcomers as "The Land of Pleasant Living" and they would call themselves "Come Heres." Natives of the Northern Neck still love their own special nook of the world and think of it as their very own, proudly calling themselves "Been Heres"!

This is my sketchbook of the difficult years that fell between the construction of the two access bridges to the Northern Neck: the era marked by the Great Depression and World War II.

I have attempted to paint a picture of life as many of the people here experienced it by including various minutiae throughout these sketches that may depict a closer portrayal of the time, along with relating many customs, events, and activities of the people.

Following the war years and the opening of the Norris Bridge, a new kind of life came to the area. The ever-changing world continues to open doors to new changes of lifestyle here in this place and, hopefully, these will always be positive developments.